"Stress and transformation are two unique concepts, but you cannot successfully manage the first without understanding and embracing the second. In this breakthrough book, longtime stress researchers Childre and Rozman show how anyone can take even the most debilitating forms of stress and transform or convert them into positive energy and feelings. The results are better performance and greater happiness in all aspects of your life. This book will change your life!"

—Charles B. Inlander, president of the People's Medical Society, coauthor of *Stress: 63 Ways to Relieve the Tension and Stay Healthy*, and cofounder of Stress Freedom United (www.stressfreedom.org).

"HeartMath has clearly proven that your heart is the major reactor to stress, the key to understanding harmony between body, mind, and emotions. Nothing is more critical to life and health than transforming stress into a positive influence. HeartMath provides that path to transformation."

—C. Norman Shealy, MD, Ph.D., founding president of the American Holistic Medical Association, president of the Holos University Graduate Seminary, author of *90 Days to Stress-Free Living*, and coauthor with Carolyn Myss of *The Creation of Health*

"*Transforming Stress* clea⌐   ⌐ader through the step-by-step process to ⌐ transforming that energ⌐ I recommend this book   ⌐⌐!"

—Hale Dwoskin, best-selling *The Sedona Me⌐*   ⌐sting *Happiness, Success, Peace, and Emotiona⌐* ⌐eing

"In these times of greatly increased perception of stress by all humans, the salvation of our species is likely to come from learning how to view the world through one's heart rather than just through one's head. Childre and Rozman's *Transforming Stress* teaches one how to do this in magnificent fashion. These are first-rate tools for self-healing and for learning how to become inner-self managed."

— William A. Tiller, professor emeritus in the Department of Materials Science at Stanford University, research scientist, author, and physicist in the film "What the Bleep Do We Know!?"

"Whether it's forgiveness or stress management, we need, in addition to sound theory, effective tools with which to achieve the desired results. This groundbreaking book gives us both. Truly a breakthrough book on health."

— Colin Tipping, author of *Radical Forgiveness: Making Room for the Miracle and Spiritual Intelligence at Work*

"When I encountered HeartMath, I felt like I had received the operating manual for life. *Transforming Stress* simply and accessibly presents the scientific rationale, as well as the practical techniques, that underlie HeartMath's proven system. If you want to learn how to live authentically from the heart in a way that gives you control over your responses to a chaotic and changing world, read this book."

— Nina Utne, chairperson of *Utne* magazine.

"With the goal of controlling stress, reducing inner tension and achieving a sense of emotional regulation, HeartMath attempts to achieve a state of inner coherence by means of heart rate variability control. The HeartMath techniques laid out by authors Childre and Rozman in their new book, *Transforming Stress*, could prove to be an extremely valuable treatment alternative to doctor- and self-prescribed medicines and drugs, along with proper diet, sleep, and exercise, in a number of complicated physical and emotional conditions like anger management and anxiety, mood, post-traumatic stress, and attention-deficit disorders."

> —William C. Torch, MD, MSc., consultant in child and adult neurology, psychiatry and sleep disorders medicine and medical director of the Neurodevelopmental, Neurodiagnostic Center and the Washoe Sleep Disorders Center, both in Reno, NV

"In today's fast-paced business world, even my most successful executive clients become overcommitted and overwhelmed. *Transforming Stress* offers easy-to-follow explanations and action steps that work for everyone. I am highly recommending this book to all of my clients!"

> —Joan Eleanor Gustafson, international marketing leader, executive coach, and professional speaker

"The business world is now often characterized by short-term and financially driven values. The outside world is increasingly characterized by ambiguity, complexity, speed, and unpredictability. It is perhaps not surprising that many individuals perceive this as threatening, which all too often leads to symptoms and conditions such as stress and anxiety. HeartMath has shown in research and case studies that there is a relationship between perception and physiology, and that we can influence both to have a significant and beneficial impact on these conditions. Few interventions have been shown to make such a positive and, equally important, sustained impact in these areas. Knowledge of HeartMath measurement techniques, monitoring strategies, and tools has transformed my clinical practice over the last few years in assisting individuals, teams, and businesses manage these costly issues."

—Tony Yardley-Jones, FFOM, FRCS (Ed), Ph.D.,
specialist in occupational medicine, London, UK

Transforming
Stress

**The HeartMath® Solution
for Relieving Worry,
Fatigue, and Tension**

Doc Childre • Deborah Rozman, Ph.D.

New Harbinger Publications, Inc.

Publisher's Note

This publication is designed to provide accurate and authoritative information in regard to the subject matter covered. It is sold with the understanding that the publisher is not engaged in rendering psychological, financial, legal, or other professional services. If expert assistance or counseling is needed, the services of a competent professional should be sought.

HeartMath, Heart Lock-In, Freeze-Frame are registered trademarks of the Institue of HeartMath.

Quick Coherence and Attitude Breathing are registered trademarks of Doc Childre.

Freeze-Frame is a registered trademarks of Quantum Intech, Inc.

Distributed in Canada by Raincoast Books.

Copyright © 2005 by Doc Childre and Deborah Rozman
New Harbinger Publications, Inc.
5674 Shattuck Avenue
Oakland, CA 94609

Cover design by Amy Shoup; Acquired by Catharine Sutker; Edited by Jessica Beebe; Text design by Michele Waters-Kermes

Library of Congress Cataloging-in-Publication Data

Childre, Doc Lew, 1945-
  Transforming stress : the HeartMath solution for relieving worry, fatigue, and tension / by Doc Childre and Deborah Rozman.
      p. cm.
  Includes bibliographical references.
  ISBN-10 1-57224-397-X
  ISBN-13 978-1-57224-397-2
  1. Stress management—Popular works. 2. Heart beat—Psychological aspects. I. Rozman, Deborah. II. Title.
  RA785.C453 2005
  155.9'042—dc22
                    2005009182

FSC
MIX
Paper
FSC® C011935

RAINFOREST ALLIANCE CERTIFIED

All Rights Reserved
Printed in the United States of America
New Harbinger Publications' website address: www.newharbinger.com

13   12   11

20   19   18   17   16   15   14

Dedication

This book is dedicated to people who are looking for a clear way to find their own emotional empowerment in today's fast-paced world. Emotional empowerment *can* be achieved, resulting in tremendous individual stress reduction. The energy saved translates into increased happiness and an increased satisfaction with oneself. This empowerment comes from the alignment of the mind and emotions with the heart's intuition. Our intention—and the goal of our research—is to make it easier for people to connect with their intuition and the power of their heart to establish inner security. As people clean up their own "stress mess," they raise their individual consciousness and the consciousness of the planetary whole: a mission that's deep within the heart of each of us, whether we know it or not.

Contents

Foreword

The word "stress" has been used in physics for hundreds of years to describe an external force that produces distortion or strain in metals. However, seven decades ago, it was redefined by the brilliant Canadian researcher Hans Selye as "the non-specific response of the body to any demand for change." At the time, it was widely believed that each disease had its own specific cause: for example, the tubercle bacillus and pneumococcus caused tuberculosis and pneumonia, and scurvy and rickets were due to specific vitamin deficiencies. What Selye proposed was just the opposite; namely, that very different physical and emotional challenges could produce the same stomach ulcerations and shrinkage of lymphoid tissue in laboratory animals. He also demonstrated that prolonged stress caused changes in other tissues similar to those seen in patients suffering from heart attacks, stroke, kidney disease, rheumatoid arthritis, and other disorders he labeled "diseases of adaptation."

Selye's speculations attracted considerable attention, and although "stress" was soon part of vernacular speech, it became a buzzword that signified different things to different people. Some used it to refer to an annoying or distressful situation (an abusive boss, the loss of a loved one), while for others it was the resultant unpleasant emotional (fear, anger, frustration) or physical (palpitations, chest pain, "agita") symptoms that were experienced. To further complicate things, people respond to the same stressful stimulus quite differently. Some blush, while others become pale or experience symptoms ranging from sweaty palms to diarrhea. In addition, things that are very distressful for some individuals can be extremely enjoyable for others, as readily illustrated by observing passengers on a steep roller-coaster ride. Some are crouched down in the back seats with their eyes shut, jaws clenched, white knuckled as they clench the retaining bar. They can't wait for the ride in the torture chamber to end so they can get away. But up front are the thrill seekers, who yell and relish every abrupt plunge, and then race to get on the very next ride! And in between, you may find a few with an air of nonchalance that seems to border on boredom. So, was the roller-coaster ride stressful?

The roller coaster is a useful analogy that helps to explain stress. What distinguished the riders in the back from those up front was the sense of control they had over the event. While neither group had any more or less control, their perceptions and expectations were quite different. Although stress is difficult to define because it is such a subjective phenomenon, all of our clinical and experimental research confirms that the perception of having no control is always distressful – and that's what stress is all about. Many times we create our own stress because of faulty perceptions. You can teach people to move from the back of the roller coaster to the front, and you can reduce stress by utilizing the techniques in this book to improve your sense of control.

Our myriad metabolic and physiologic fight-or-flight responses to stress have been exquisitely honed over the lengthy course of human evolution as lifesaving measures. The fact that these occur automatically and instantaneously suggests a coordinated system of communication throughout the body that is difficult to comprehend. Our current concept of communication visualizes chemical messengers fitting into specialized receptor sites on cell walls like keys that only open certain locks. However, such physical structural matching of molecules that could only occur on a random collision basis cannot explain the vast multitude of diverse stress responses that happen all over the body in milliseconds. An emerging paradigm of communication at a physical/atomic level that includes electromagnetic signaling seems much more likely, especially since all molecular messages are ultimately transmitted to the interior of the cell by weak energy signals that activate or inhibit various enzyme systems. Messenger molecules emit specific frequencies that may serve as a means of communication, much like a radio, which receives waveforms carrying specific information only from the station to which it is tuned to coresonate and to none other. In this analogy, one can visualize an AM, FM, or shortwave transmitter with the capability of sending an infinite number of signals that simultaneously reach specific sites throughout the body to stimulate numerous diverse fight-or-flight responses.

The ancients believed that the heart rather than the brain was the seat of emotion. HeartMath research has demonstrated that the magnetic field of the heart is much more powerful than the brain and can influence not only our own brain waves but also those of individuals several feet away. There is good evidence that cell walls may also have receptor sites for feeble electromagnetic signals that can produce the same facilitating and inhibiting effects as molecular messengers. Thus, EEG and ECG waves may not simply represent the noise of the machinery of the brain or heart but rather signals being sent to different sites in the body.

This type of subtle energy communication within the body provides solid scientific support for the groundbreaking HeartMath solution for transforming stress. What is unique about this approach is the ability to control internal conversations so that the disjointed dialogue seen during stress is transformed into communication that becomes coherent, concordant, and congruous. Good health depends on good communication — good communication within *and* without. Practicing the HeartMath approach will improve your ability to communicate more effectively and harmoniously, internally as well as with others. It also confirms that the body is its own best pharmacy and provides an opportunity to tap into the vast innate power of self-healing that resides in all of us.

The closest Chinese word for stress consists of two characters; one signifies "danger" and the other "opportunity." *Transforming Stress* allows you to make that choice by teaching you how to harness stress so that you can become more productive, rather than self-destructive.

—Paul J. Rosch, MD, FACP
President, The American Institute of Stress
Clinical Professor of Medicine and
Psychiatry, New York Medical College

Acknowledgments

We would like to acknowledge the many people who have contributed to this book, *Transforming Stress,* which is a result of over thirty years of dedicated research and practice. We want to thank the entire staff of the HeartMath companies, who have made transforming stress an important part of their workplace culture and have made it their mission to bring these techniques and tools to people all over the world. We would like to thank our clients for their sincere practice of the HeartMath tools and for the many narratives they gave us explaining how their lives and the lives of people around them have been enriched as a result. We wish there had been room in the book to share more of their powerful stories of transformation. We also appreciate the scientific researchers we have referenced and others who are building a foundation for understanding the role of stress in the human system and how it affects people's well-being.

We especially want to thank Dr. Paul Rosch, president of the American Institute of Stress, who has worked tirelessly since 1978 to raise awareness among the scientific community and the general public that stress is America's number one health problem. The American Institute of Stress, founded by noted stress researcher Hans Selye, who coined the term "stress" as it is used today, is dedicated to advancing our understanding of the role of stress in health and illness, the nature and importance of the mind-body relationship, and our inherent and immense potential for self-healing. We are honored that Dr. Rosch wrote the foreword to this book and serves as a member of the scientific advisory board of the Institute of HeartMath and the medical advisory board of Quantum Intech, Inc.

Finally, we want to acknowledge those who facilitated this book: Matt McKay, Catharine Sutker, and others at New Harbinger Publications who asked us to write the book out of recognition of the world's need for scientifically validated, in-the-moment solutions for stress relief; Dr. Rollin McCraty, director of research at the Institute of HeartMath for his assistance with scientific explanations; Dana Tomasino, researcher at the Institute of HeartMath for her assistance with references; Euphrasia Carroll and Priscilla Stuckey, our development editors; and Jessica Beebe, our copyeditor. Their help and care is much appreciated.

Introduction

Transforming Stress is a research-based, hopeful answer to a malady of modern times: unremitting and increasing levels of stress. The statistics on mounting stress and its detrimental effects on body, mind, emotions, and health shout at us. The American Institute of Stress notes that 75 to 90 percent of visits to primary care physicians are for stress-related complaints (Rosch 1991). A Harvard study shows that people who live in a state of high anxiety are four and a half times more likely to suffer sudden cardiac death than nonanxious individuals (Kawachi et al. 1994). An international investigation reveals that people who are unable to effectively manage their stress have a 40 percent higher death rate than their nonstressed counterparts (Eysenck 1988). These statistics are over ten years old, and as stress has mounted in our fast-paced society, are likely to be higher now.

In 2002, people in the United States bought nearly $17.2 billion worth of antidepressants and antianxiety drugs, up more than 10 percent from 2001. Americans spent $1.1 billion in the same year on just two of the major prescription sleeping pills, to say nothing of the over-the-counter brands, and seven of the top ten best-selling drugs are for stress-related ailments (NDCHealth 2003).

A poll conducted by *Cosmopolitan* magazine found that stress is an epidemic among women ages eighteen to twenty-nine: 66 percent say they feel a "considerable to moderate" amount of stress daily, and 54 percent say their stress level has increased in the last year (Colino 2004). Developed nations across the globe report higher levels of stress, anger, anxiety, and dissatisfaction at work than ever before. CNN reports that a survey conducted by the Society for Human Resource Professionals found that in the United States, eight out of ten people want to find another job (Haggin Geary 2003). The statistics scream: *Too much stress hurts.* It hurts relationships and work performance. It hurts health and quality of life. It hurts your enjoyment of yourself, others, and life.

The problem is that stress has become all pervasive. Faster communications speed up events and people's sense of time. There is more to do than time to do it. Millions are bombarded with a constant stream of information. They are exposed to other people's heightened stress at home, at school, and in the workplace, with little respite. People broadcast their stress through reactions, energies, and words, and everyone feels it. Many are so stressed they feel they don't have time to deal with stress. The momentum of stress carries people with it.

It's time to wake up and do something. Regardless of economic boom or recession, miracle drugs, or technological conveniences, stress levels keep rising. People keep doing the same things that stress them as if there's nothing they can do about it. Stress is at the root of so many personal, family, health, workplace, and social problems, but there's no societal movement to stop it. Stress can become so habit-forming that it numbs your brain to the urgency of addressing it, making you oblivious to the obvious. Most people try to deal with the effects and ignore the cause. It's easy to forget that stress is the body's warning signal that something is out of whack and delude yourself into thinking that it's normal.

When you become accustomed to the stimulation of stress, ongoing tension, strain, and worry start to seem normal. After all, most people you know feel this way. Their workloads and pressures are so intense they believe they can't take time to deal with stress. The boss expects them to produce more, the kids have a lot of stress from school and peer pressure, there are always more bills to pay, and there is an unrelenting pressure to buy or do. The world is in transition, with terror reports and heightened alerts, and people don't know where it's headed. This creates a gnawing insecurity and for many a hopeless resignation. It's time for ividuals to take charge and do something. It's time for genuine action.

Your Heart Really Knows

Genuine care is a powerful weapon against galloping stress. When people are in extreme situations, they often "go to the heart" to try to see what to do. The heart is both a physical organ and an intuitive feeling center, as we'll show throughout this book. The heart is the central rhythmic force that affects other rhythms throughout your body, which in turn affect your resilience. The human body is, in fact, tremendously resilient. And this offers a great stress-reducing resource. For example, you can see quick recovery from stress in young children when they don't get their way. One minute they're emotionally upset, and the very next minute they're back in their heart, laughing and playing. Most people, as they grow older, lose that emotional flexibility to release and let go, so stress accumulates. Your mind and brain hold on to past fears and disappointments and project future ones. Your emotions stay drained, and your nervous system stays strained. You get trapped in your stresses. When this happens, your heart feels dismayed and your spirit feels constricted.

It takes deeper intelligence to stop the stress momentum once and for all. While there are no quick fixes, you can take effective, long-lasting steps once you start listening to your heart. Your heart really knows what to do, but it helps to first understand what keeps you caught up in the momentum of stress.

How Stress Affects You

The lack of understanding of how to address emotions is the primary cause of today's stress epidemic. People believe that the mind rules. But more often than not, it's the emotions that determine choices and behaviors.

Stress affects people in different ways. Stress can create a dynamic or creative challenge, if you approach it positively and don't get too far out of balance. Too much stress creates overload; your creativity and clarity decline, and you feel disconnected from yourself. You experience stress overload as aches and pains, fragmented thinking, negative attitudes, and feeling out of control. But these are secondary responses. Where you first experience stress is in your *feeling world*. This is the space within yourself where you register feelings and moods. There is a lot of information contained in your feeling world, just as there is in your mind, and this information can be very useful to you. But you have to know how to read your feelings. Stress often starts with a feeling. You first feel the tension, irritation, or worry, and then it escalates into stronger emotions of frustration, anxiety, or anger. Finally, you end up overloaded and exhausted.

You accumulate stress when you carry around feelings of stress without resolving them. Feelings aren't bad or wrong. You just may not fully understand what they are trying to tell you. Many feelings can cause stress: fear, worry, sadness, loneliness, edginess, reactivity, irritation, anger, boredom, moodiness, hurt, jealousy, guilt, greed, envy, resentment. You can probably think of others.

In our society, people don't like to acknowledge feelings. If you admit to yourself that your emotions are managing you, rather than the other way around, you may fear you are lesser, incapable, or even crazy. If you're like most people, you don't like to admit you're hurting or feeling bad, that emotions are running you ragged, or that you feel a slow burn inside. You'd rather ignore it, squish it, hide it, or take it out on others. When emotions have nowhere to go, the emotional energy builds up and then gets vented in judgment, projection, or blame. If you can't find relief, you may blow up or want to go hide under the covers. This is often called the "fight-or-flight" response. Stress switches on brain circuits and hormones that prepare the body to protect itself in dangerous situations. The problem is this survival circuitry gets activated by everyday situations that are stressful but not life-threatening—an argument with your mate, a traffic jam, a looming deadline—until your mind, emotions, and body are on stress overload. It doesn't have to be this way.

Most people have heard about ways to cope with stress—eating nutritious foods, drinking less alcohol and coffee, stopping smoking, exercising, meditating, taking breaks, spending time with friends, and doing fun things—but they rarely get around to following the advice or do so sporadically. Let's face it: Changing habits is inconvenient, especially if you gain comfort from eating fatty or sugary foods or carbs, or feel less stress after drinking coffee or smoking. Few people want to eliminate pleasures from their life, even in the name of stopping stress. Plus, most people are moving so fast on their stress treadmill that they don't see how they can afford the luxury of exercise or enough relaxation time to make a difference. Time is like money; there's never enough. The nagging feeling that you're never caught up keeps you from doing the things you know you should.

If this sounds like you, you're not alone, and this book is written especially for you. There is a new, more effective approach that thousands of people just like you are using to let go of stress and take better care of themselves, their families, and their jobs. It doesn't address your lifestyle habits head-on, because that's just putting a Band-Aid on the problem. Instead, it transforms your underlying stress and makes it easier for you to let go of unhealthy behaviors. You'll feel better because you *are* better.

The HeartMath Solution to Stress

Fortunately, new research shows that you can stop the momentum of stress and create more inner peace, whatever your circumstances. You don't have to succumb to ongoing stress. Exciting new research on the heart has found that there is a way to relieve stress that both comforts you and—most importantly—*transforms* stress into healthy, positive feelings and creative energy.

To "transform" means to change in nature or substance—to change one thing into another, like a frog transformed into a prince or a caterpillar to a butterfly. To "transform" also means to alter voltage and current by means of an electrical transformer. A transformer uses electromagnetic current to transfer electrical energy from one circuit to another. All of these definitions apply to transforming stress, even the last one. That's because the physical heart can be used as a transformer to repattern your stress circuitry. In fact, the heart sends signals to the brain that help you transform your stress responses far more quickly than was thought possible. We'll be teaching you how in this book.

Transforming Stress isn't just another stress management or coping system. It's revolutionary. It shows you how to transform emotional and mental energy into new, satisfying feelings and intelligent perceptions that ease the stress. It goes to the heart of the matter to give you power over the automatic stress responses that have become etched into your neural circuitry. Through the heart, you can transform the physiology of stress into the physiology of quick recovery, increased energy, and new insight. This helps slow the effects of aging by bringing you closer to the emotional flexibility you had as a child.

The HeartMath approach to transforming worry, fatigue, and tension has been scientifically validated and successfully applied by people around the world on five continents. From providing stress-reduction programs and before-and-after assessments for thousands of people, the HeartMath training company, HeartMath LLC, is in a position to take the pulse of stress in many environments: corporations, hospitals, government agencies, schools, sports and fitness centers, with health professionals, teachers, children, and other individuals. Many people write to us about how they have used HeartMath methods to successfully transform their stress and achieve their goals. Some learned HeartMath methods from employer-sponsored programs, some from a book or learning program, and others from coaching by a HeartMath provider.

How to Use This Book

In this book, you will read success stories from people like you. (In some cases, their names have been changed at their request to protect their privacy.) You will learn key tools and techniques that they practiced. You will pinpoint your key stressors and then use the tools to change your emotional responses to them. You will see why health professionals teach these techniques and tools to clients.

Throughout this book, we'll offer exercises to help deepen your understanding of the HeartMath techniques. Use a journal or a notebook to record your responses to the exercises and to keep track of new perceptions and intuitive insights you gain from using the tools and techniques. Writing will help you remember to act on these insights. You may be tempted to skip the exercises and keep reading, but you'll find that you get much more out of this book if you pause to do them.

The HeartMath techniques can be used on the spot, right when you feel your stress temperature rising. No one needs to know you're using them. Within moments, you will release tension, worry, and frustration. You will think more clearly, and intuitive insight will be more available to you. You will see how to get off your stress treadmill. You will feel better and do better.

In this book, you will learn how to

- stop emotional energy drains

- stop judging others or yourself

- stop trying to live up to others' unrealistic expectations of you

- gain new energy and vitality

- take charge of your life

- experience the joy of more stress-free living

- become who you really want to be at work, at home, and with yourself

The HeartMath solution helps you refill your emotional energy coffers. Wouldn't you rather have positive feelings flowing through your system throughout the day—feelings like care, strength, courage, kindness, warmth, appreciation, sincerity, and fun? Wouldn't you rather move through your busy days feeling energized and authentic, able to say no when you need to and yes when you really can?

With each HeartMath tool you use, you recharge your emotional batteries. You replace emotional drain with emotional gain. You give yourself back your authentic self and your self-respect. What's more, you give yourself more creative intelligence. You see how to communicate more effectively, and others respect you more. You become your real self, connecting with your primary source of intuition and power. These are just some of the stress relief benefits you will find as you use the HeartMath solution.

chapter 1

A Change of Heart Changes Everything

More than thirty years ago, a young man was at a crossroads. He had grown up hearing that the heart was where you'd find wisdom and fulfillment. Now he needed to determine whether this was true or not. He saw that societal changes were straining people's ability to cope, and, out of a deep care, he wanted to find a simple system by which people could empower themselves to increase their well-being.

This is how Doc Childre, one of the authors of this book, began his research into stress and performance— research that would grow into dozens of scientific papers and books on the role of the heart in human physiology and well-being. He started by studying different philosophical, religious, and psychological systems and realized that the unifying factor among the various traditions and beliefs was the idea that the "heart" was the center of intuition and connection to others. So he decided to find out what this "heart" really was and to research it as a possible key to transforming stress.

The Heart in HeartMath

People commonly use the word "heart" in two senses. There is the physical heart, with its rhythmic contractions that pump blood throughout the body. And then there is the metaphorical heart, which we refer to when we say, "Listen to your heart," "Have a heart," or "Speak from your heart." The heart symbolizes the center or core, as in "getting to the heart of the matter."

Doc decided to research the physical heart in conjunction with the metaphorical heart. He gathered together engineers, psychologists, medical researchers, educators, and businesspeople as a human "lab." He invited them to test simple techniques to listen to the heart, and then measured and analyzed the data. In 1991, when they had replicable results, Doc founded the nonprofit Institute of HeartMath to further investigate the heart and its role in the human system. His goal was to develop a simple, straightforward, step-by-step system of scientifically validated tools—a way that anyone could reliably listen to and follow the heart as a source of intelligence. He called it the "math" of the heart, or HeartMath. The "math" meant equations, psychological equations. As in, *Act this way, and this will result.* Like $1 + 1 = 2$.

While Doc was doing his early research, Deborah Rozman was studying attitude change theory, first at the University of Chicago, then at University of California, Santa Cruz. She developed a method in which clients would listen to what their head had to say, then listen to what their heart had to say about the same issues. She saw how dramatically different the two domains were, and she sought to develop a new psychology to understand the wisdom of the heart. Debbie was introduced to Doc's theories of heart intelligence in the mid-1980s and realized this was her next step. Impressed by his deep understanding of the heart and human nature, she joined forces with Doc and others to research heart-brain dynamics and emotions.

As we write this book, well over a decade after the launch of the Institute of HeartMath research lab, many exciting discoveries about the heart have been made, both by our lab and by other institutes. We will touch on just a few in this book.

Emotions and Heart Rhythms

When we started the lab, our first research objective was to see if we could find any correlation whatsoever between the physical heart and people's emotional states. When the heart beats, it produces a wave of pressure which we feel as the pulse. Chinese medical doctors have long known that the pulse contains information about the emotional and physical health of the body.

One of our first efforts was to study the *electrocardiogram,* or ECG, which measures changes in the electrical potentials occurring during the heartbeat, when people were in different emotional states. Cardiologists, for example, had reported noticing a difference in the ECG of people with a history of emotional stress (Huang, Ebey, and Wolf 1989). So we hooked people up to ECG recorders and analyzed their ECG while they experienced different emotions. We found that strong negative emotional states did in fact change the shape of the ECG. The search was on for ECG patterns that would show other emotional states and reveal more subtle changes in positive and negative emotions. After experimenting with numerous methods of analyzing the ECG, we found that the pattern of the heart rhythm reflected a person's emotional state better than any other heart, skin, or brain measures we'd seen.

We'd also looked at *heart rate* (the number of times the heart beats in a minute), but it did not accurately reflect emotional state. However, heart rate changes with every heartbeat, and by analyzing the beat-to-beat changes (called *heart rate variability* or *heart rhythm analysis*), we found gold. We found that the pattern of beat-to-beat changes reflected emotional state changes. We had discovered a critical link between emotional states and the rhythms of the heart. The results of this breakthrough were first published in the *American Journal of Cardiology* in 1995 by McCraty and colleagues.

Emotions Determine Heart Rhythms

Our studies found that positive and uplifting emotional states, such as sincere love, care, compassion, and appreciation, create a smooth and ordered heart rhythm pattern, like figure 1.1. In physics, this harmonious pattern is called a *sine wave,* or *coherent waveform.* And subjects felt more harmonious and coherent when their heart rhythms were coherent. On the other hand, negative or stressful emotional states, such as anger, frustration, worry, and anxiety, create jagged, disordered heart rhythm patterns, like figure 1.2 (McCraty et al. 1995; Tiller, McCraty, and Atkinson 1996). This is called an *incoherent waveform* and looks similar to an earthquake graph. When people feel strong negative emotions, they often are incoherent or feel like there's an earthquake going on inside. The disturbed feeling is what incoherence feels like.

You Can Change Your Heart Rhythm Patterns

The majority of people believe that emotions just "happen" to them. HeartMath research has found that people have much more power over their emotional well-being than they give themselves credit for. They just don't know how to access that power. They need to learn how to do it (McCraty and Childre 2002).

Figure 1.1   **Figure 1.2**

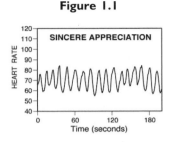
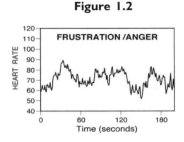

© *Copyright Institute of HeartMath*

Figure 1.1 shows the heart rate variability or heart rhythm pattern typical of appreciation and other positive feelings. This smooth heart rhythm is what scientists call a *highly ordered* or *coherent* pattern and is a sign of good health and emotional balance.

Figure 1.2 shows the irregular, jerky heart rhythm pattern typical of stressful feelings like anger, frustration, worry, and anxiety. This is called an *incoherent* pattern.

Everyone talks about positive and negative emotions, but few scientists have studied the impact that different emotional states have on the body. Until a few years ago, there were only a handful of studies on positive emotions. Most research has focused on pathological behaviors or on the effects of disturbed emotions, such as hostility, depression, anxiety, and stress on the body.

At the HeartMath lab, we discovered a window into the heart—both the physical heart and the metaphorical heart of feeling that poets, philosophers, religions, and motivational speakers refer to. When you act on the sayings, "Play from your heart" or "Put your heart into it," you change your heart rhythm pattern and your physiology. Your heart rhythms, nervous system, immune system, and hormonal system respond differently. Coherent heart rhythms and positive emotions enhance the immune response, improve hormonal and nervous system balance, and alleviate pain (Rein, Atkinson, and McCraty 1995; McCraty et al. 1996; McCraty, Barrios-Choplin, et al. 1998; McCraty and Atkinson 2003; McCraty and Childre 2004). Understanding how to apply this discovery is an essential step in developing your power to transform stress.

Positive Emotions Can Transform Your Brain, Body, and Life

The research did not stop there. We found that positive emotions and smooth heart rhythm patterns facilitate *cortical* or *higher brain* function, whereas stressful emotions and disordered heart rhythms inhibit a person's ability to coherently organize thoughts or reason clearly (McCraty and Atkinson 2003). This helps explain why when people feel stressed, they make more mistakes and say or do things they later regret.

The lab also discovered that the electromagnetic field generated by the heart changes according to the heart rhythm pattern. The heart's field extends outside the body and can be measured across the room (McCraty 2004). You are literally making waves as you feel different emotions, and those waves affect the people around you.

We now refer to the combination of physical heart and emotion as the *energetic heart*. What we mean is that the heart's electromagnetic field acts as a carrier of the pattern and energy of what we are feeling. We tell children, "Be genuine from the heart," "Sing from the heart," and "Do your best from the heart," because we know that energy positively expressed from the heart helps. When someone feels genuine compassion or sincerely wants to forgive, there's a heartfelt prompting and then the mind (brain) takes that feeling and spreads it throughout the body. That heartfelt energetic place is where the physical and feeling heart meet to give you more intent and *heart power.*

HeartMath techniques transform stress because they show you how to engage the power of your heart to change your heart rhythm pattern and your emotions right in the moment. While some people have stronger tendencies toward optimism or pessimism, based on genetics, environment, or the activity of neurotransmitters or hormones, we have found that anyone can learn to change their physiology and their emotions through the power of the heart.

If you had a heart rhythm monitor with a pulse sensor, you could watch your heart rhythm pattern change in real time as you change your thoughts and feelings by using a HeartMath technique. The Freeze-Framer software, which we'll talk about in chapter 10, is designed to give you this objective feedback. The HeartMath techniques you will learn in this book train you to listen to your own heart sensations or heart signals. By becoming attuned to your heart sensations, you learn to understand their meaning to you. Your heart sensations give you signals, like a traffic light: *stop, go, caution.* When your heart rhythms are smooth and coherent, you feel a sense of solidity and security. This is your heart signaling *Yes, go.* When you're feeling frustrated, anxious, or stressed and your heart rhythms are jagged and incoherent, you're getting a red light. These stressful feelings are cues to stop and reevaluate. This is your opportunity to use a HeartMath tool to manage your emotions, change your heart rhythms, and shift your perceptions. Transforming stress involves learning how to listen to your heart signals.

When you are stressed, if you connect with your energetic heart and change your heart rhythm to a more ordered and coherent pattern, your feelings and perceptions will change. Coherent heart rhythms help activate feelings of security and calm that bring your thoughts into more coherence. An ordered or coherent heart rhythm increases synchronization of the brain's electrical rhythms with the electrical rhythms of the heart (McCraty and Atkinson 2003). You need this increased heart-brain synchronization to gain new perspectives. By generating a positive emotion or attitude to increase heart-brain synchronization, you aren't denying or brushing aside underlying stress. You're getting coherent and bringing in new, intelligent perspectives. Coherence expands your perception of the stressful situation, giving you more insight to make better decisions. You not only feel better, you do better. A change of heart changes everything.

Harnessing the Power of the Heart

The key to transforming stress lies in your power to regulate your emotions and perceptions. That power comes from your heart. You can learn how to engage your heart rhythms to manage your emotions and perceptions, even when they are flaring, and bring your system back to inner harmony. You don't manage the situation, which may be beyond your control. You manage your reaction to it, gaining a new feeling with new insight about how to best approach the stressful situation even as it is occurring. Beginning in the next chapter, we'll teach you the tools and techniques to do this for yourself. Before you know it, you'll be transforming stress in your own life.

chapter 2

The Rhythm of Emotion

Rhythm makes music harmonious or chaotic, a dancer grace-
ful or awkward, and life smooth or rough. You can release a
lot of stress by going straight to the feelings underlying it,
then regulating your emotions and heart rhythms. In doing
so, you'll learn a new rhythm of dissolving stress and moving
through resistances or rough situations as they arise.

Stress comes from *perception* and your reactions to your
perception. If you didn't perceive that an upcoming deadline
would be hard to make, it wouldn't be a stressor, and you
wouldn't feel frustrated. You might say, "Yeah, but it's a real
deadline, and I just don't have enough time." When you go
to your heart and find a new rhythm, you often find a new
perception or solution that makes the situation less over-
whelming, and the stress goes away. Or your reaction
changes, even though the situation doesn't change, and you
make peace with it.

Stressors can come from inside: feeling pressured, feeling you don't want to do something, feeling overwhelmed,
and so forth. Or they can come from outside: the traffic light
is holding you back, your teenager is giving you the cold
shoulder, your coworker is blocking you from getting things
done, the future of your job is uncertain, and so on. Either
way, you'll have an easier time when you engage the power

of your heart to regulate the underlying feelings and find a new rhythm through it all. This will brighten your attitude and boost your sense of accomplishment, your relationships, your work performance and satisfaction, and of course benefit your health. In a study of 5,716 middle-aged people, those with the highest self-regulation abilities (including managing stress and unhealthy attitudes) were over fifty times more likely to be alive and without chronic disease fifteen years later than those with the lowest self-regulation scores (Grossarth-Maticek and Eysenck 1995).

The Power of Rhythm

The power of rhythm isn't in thinking; it's in feelings and attitudes. As you bring more coherence to your heart rhythms and emotional state, you open up intuitive intelligence—especially when you need it most. Emotions can move faster than thoughts, and they bias your perceptions and thought. As you apply heart power to transform your emotions, you can start to see how this works in yourself.

 Try this. Put your hand on your heart, in the center of your chest, and find a sincere feeling of appreciation for someone or something in your life (a person, place, or pet, for example). Choose something that's easy to appreciate, with no negative emotional history to color your appreciation. Feel that appreciation from your heart for twenty to thirty seconds. Notice any changes in your feeling world or perceptions compared to before this exercise. This is the energetic heart in action.

This brief moment of sincere appreciation has probably changed your heart rhythms and given you more sensitivity to your feeling world. It may have even given you some intuitive perception and clarity. By increasing your heart rhythm coherence, you connect with your intuition. You can learn to change your heart rhythm to gain new insight. Insight comes faster as you increase your emotional management skills. You can learn to be your real self, listening to your heart — your fundamental source of power and intuition — to regulate the emotions. We call this *listening to heart intelligence.*

Heart intelligence is the flow of new awareness and intuition that you experience once the mind and emotions are brought into coherent alignment with the heart. It can be activated through self-initiated practice. You experience heart intelligence as direct, intuitive knowing that manifests in thoughts and emotions that benefit you and others and guide you in behaviors that smooth your way through life. Everyone has this coherent intelligence within, waiting to be uncovered.

Heart intelligence doesn't have to be a mystery. We hear people telling others to use heart intelligence all the time. When you tell children to remember to appreciate, or tell a friend to be honest with himself, or tell someone to follow her heart, these are suggestions of heart intelligence. When you tell someone who's holding on to resentment about the past, "It's time to forgive," or "You have to release and let go of that stuff," that's a sincere gesture of heart intelligence. You will find a whole realm of examples if you start looking for them. They point to a way of living life from the energetic heart zone, not just going to your heart when you're down and out. By living from the heart more, you connect with intuitive guidance more consistently, and that's what gives you rhythm through stress resistances.

Too often, people talk about the heart only when talking about children, love, and flowers. It's time to focus not on the *sentiment* of the heart but on the *intelligence* of the heart. The heart offers a way to go deeper to find answers. It is heartfelt intent that generates change in people. It is the power of the heart that gives momentum to your chosen direction, and it is the intuitive intelligence of the heart that guides you on the way.

Emotional Regeneration

One attitude shift—connecting with your heart power and intelligence when you feel emotional turmoil or stress—is a small energy investment with big energy savings. It creates *emotional regeneration* by giving you a reserve of high-quality emotional energy you can use to change what you thought you couldn't or find ease with what you can't yet change.

High-quality emotional energy is like high-octane gas for smoother and faster mental performance. That's why people's hearts often prompt them to say, "Let's sleep on it" when they have to make a decision and their energy is low. Coherent emotional energy is the fuel that powers clear intuition. You intuitively know you can't make the best decisions when your emotions are disturbed or your energy is drained. When your emotional energy reserves are low, the activity of your nervous system becomes incoherent and unregulated, which decreases clarity and hinders your ability to evaluate situations and make effective decisions. Emotional energy also provides the firing power for carrying out your intentions.

> *Dave describes it well. "Whenever something at work or home would go awry—and this happens often—I'd feel the stress crunch of tension, worry, then fatigue. The stress stayed with me until some patchwork solution appeared, then things would ease up. Every day was herky-jerky like that. Now that I'm using HeartMath tools, problems still give me that initial tension, but there's a new rhythm that doesn't take me out or bring me down emotionally. I think more clearly through the process."*

You become more efficient in emotional regeneration as you overcome old patterns. It's a process, and your ratio of effort to reward will gradually increase. At first, you might take three steps forward and two steps back, but you're still going forward, and you can feel the difference. With more practice, you might take three steps forward and one step back. By acknowledging that progress happens through increasing ratios, you allow yourself latitude in the learning process. You assess your ratios of progress rather than expecting yourself to be perfect all the time.

The capacity for emotional regeneration allows you to recoup faster after a stressful episode and buffer yourself from future stressors. Emotional regeneration has a quality of peace and buoyancy. You are more upbeat and energetic, ready for any challenge, and you handle the challenges with more poise. It's not a state you pump yourself up for, and it's not a false optimism. It comes from a genuine feeling or knowing that you are connected to your heart intelligence.

How do you find this genuine feeling or knowing? It comes naturally when you feel a love for what you're doing or an appreciation for life, or feel kindness toward someone. Try to remember a time when you've experienced these genuine feelings before. Perhaps you felt lifted above the fray, able to cope without falling prey to the stress around you.

When you learn how to build up a reserve of positive emotional energy, then emotional regeneration becomes a natural state, similar to what you felt as a child or see in young children. It's a state that releases rigidity of body and mind. Emotional regeneration reverses premature aging, mentally and physically. It also changes your perspective (McCraty and Childre 2002). Here's how.

When you're worried and overwhelmed, or when you feel emotionally drained, that pile of papers on your desk looks impossible and out of control. You think you'll never get all that work done. When you're feeling appreciative and emotionally regenerated, that pile of papers looks different: you feel confident that you can do the work easily and well. The more coherent you are, literally, the more easily it gets done. Even time seems to slow to work in your favor. That's because you have shifted into a different emotional rhythm.

Your Body Chemistry

Building up your emotional energy reserves releases different neurotransmitters, hormones, and other biochemicals in your brain and body that enhance emotional and physical regeneration. Your internal pharmacy is based on the mixture of feelings running through your body. According to Northwestern University's Donald A. Norman, author of *The Psychology of Everyday Things*, in an interview with *Scientific American*, "Emotion, or 'affect,' is an information processing system, similar to but distinct from cognition. . . . The affective system pumps neurotransmitters into the brain, changing how the brain works. You actually think differently when you are anxious than when you are happy" (Gibbs 2004, 37–37A).

Regenerating yourself emotionally helps you create a new internal pharmacy. You feel better emotionally, and you increase your intelligence—not necessarily standard IQ, but intelligence that guides you in dealing with difficult people or situations, an intuitive intelligence based on new awareness.

You can emotionally regenerate in three ways: building ① emotional energy, ② stopping emotional drains, and clearing ③ old emotional accounts. Together, these three ways build emotional resiliency to transform stress.

① *Building Emotional Energy Reserves*

The first pathway to emotional regeneration starts with learning what adds to your emotional energy. This means finding out what gives you an emotional boost without giving you an emotional letdown afterward. Coffee, sugar, and other stimulants can pick up your emotional energy, but they give only a temporary boost. You feel up for a while, and then a feeling of drain comes. Most people have to keep adding new stimulation, or they feel let down very quickly. Adding stimulants keeps adrenaline running through your system. Too much adrenaline eventually leads to exhaustion, and once you're exhausted, it gets harder and harder to find something to pick you back up. You can't build emotional reserves on adrenaline. Adrenaline also tends to intensify emotional reactions, so stress escalates.

Temporary Boosters

Millions of people use sugar, carbohydrates, or fatty foods to feel temporarily emotionally nourished, but when they look in the mirror, they feel disappointed in themselves, and stress builds. Millions also shop to feel high but then feel drained from overstimulation. On top of that, they get upset at having spent too much or having bought things they didn't need. Millions more overwork to feel a sense of accomplishment or to get praise, which feeds them emotionally for a short time, but eventually the workload catches up with them and they get overwhelmed and stressed. Up and down they go, and their stress levels keep rising.

Many people take vacations, get massages, eat health foods, or take vitamins and minerals to relieve stress or boost energy. These approaches may be effective in the short term, but very often the same old stress feelings soon prevail. That's because these are all external energy boosters. They depend on external factors. There's nothing wrong with external boosters, but they won't relieve stress for long. Even relaxation techniques or exercise routines that don't depend on external factors often provide only temporary relief. When a stress pattern is deeply rooted, it takes a different approach to change it. More stress-free living can be accomplished through practices and tools that help you operate from the energetic heart.

Sustainable Boosters

The most powerful energy boosters are the feelings that we all want more of: feelings like appreciation, genuine care, compassion, kindness, forgiveness, and love. These heartfelt feelings are internal energy boosters. They add high-quality energy to your emotional bank account. They regenerate and sustain you mentally, emotionally, and physically, even when external boosters aren't available.

You can transform stress quickly when these uplifting feelings—and the biochemicals they generate—are coursing through your body. They create hormonal mixtures that nourish your cells and your mind, prevent fatigue, and slow aging. You perceive new solutions, and you don't feel drained later. Emotional regeneration comes from having more of these positive feelings flowing through your system. Engaging the coherent power of your heart and brain to generate and sustain more of these beneficial feelings can bring you more peace and fulfillment while transforming your stress.

 So let's get started. In your notebook or journal, list five things you do to boost your emotional energy or nourish yourself emotionally. Are they external or internal energy boosters?

Stopping Emotional Drains

The second pathway to emotional regeneration is plugging leaks where your emotional energy tends to drain away. You know—the things that trigger feelings of irritation and frustration, or worry and letdown. These feelings are cues that emotional energy will be lost unless you intervene, and you easily can once you know how. Learning to track feelings that are triggers will help you see how often you let reactions like blame, hurt, and resignation prick holes in your emotional energy reserve.

The trigger feeling often starts with an "irk" or "ugh," or a dart of insecurity or envy. We all have these feelings. It's only human. They aren't bad feelings. It's what you do with them that matters. If you let insecurity take over, it's as if you've opened the spigot on your emotional energy tank, allowing worry or fear to run freely and flood your thoughts and feelings. If you let a feeling of irritation build, you end up in frustration or anger, which drains huge amounts of emotional energy. When you allow moans and groans to go unattended, thoughts of *By now this should be different* or *It's so unfair* or *That's just the way it is*—along with feelings of blame, resignation, and then depression—will sap your emotional strength.

If you pay attention, you can feel the wave of heaviness as emotional energy drains away. But most people only notice a leak when their emotional energy reserves have dropped to the point that they are cranky and fatigued, or feel down in the dumps, or have physical aches and pains. Aches and pains are warning signals telling you something is overstressed and needs attention. Whether emotional or physical, lingering pain drains what's left of your emotional energy, then saps your brain power. Research shows that chronic stress shrinks the *hippocampus,* or memory center in the brain, and chronic pain keeps the brain so occupied that it actually shrinks the entire brain (Sapolsky 1996; Melton 2004).

Track Your Triggers

You can start restoring your emotional energy by tracking your stress feelings that trigger emotional drain and then using one of the techniques you will learn in this book to transform the stress. Tracking your emotional sound effects is an enlightening exercise that gives you more awareness of your feelings and perceptions. Your outer sound effects, such as sighs, swear words, negative humor, and expressions whispered under your breath, can give you clues to the feelings underneath. Even when you don't express your feelings aloud, there is an inner emotional sound track. Your internal sound effects, like ughs or irks or groans, will influence your next thoughts and choices, and your energy level. They create an inner tone and attitude. Once you become more conscious of your inner and outer sound effects and track the feelings that are going on underneath, you'll start to see where your energy is going. You'll even see humor in your reactions, and that helps release stress too.

 In your notebook, list your most common stress feelings that drain your energy. Remember, you are trying to identify your reactions, not the situations that cause them. But identifying the situations can help you track the feelings. So make three columns: one for common situations that drain your energy, another for stress feelings you have frequently, and the third to write down the emotional sound effects (inner and outer) you use to express these feelings. You'll refer to these columns when you start practicing the tools and techniques to stop your emotional drains.

Clearing Old Emotional Accounts

The third way to replenish emotional reserves is to clear out old emotional accounts. By old emotional accounts, we mean stored-up feelings or beliefs about past events that cause you to react to current situations with more stress than you would otherwise. In other words, you have developed an emotional habit.

A lot of stress triggers and reactions are simply emotional habits. The good news is that they are habits you can change. For example, you feel irked, and you automatically fly off the handle with blame and anger. You feel worried, and you start whining at someone or cursing yourself. What's happened is that you've tapped into an old emotional account and are reacting out of habit.

Let's say an account was created when you felt disrespected by a family member. Each time that relative calls, you feel irritated. Your account is overloaded with accumulated irritation toward that relative. The stored irritation keeps you reacting in the same old way, over and over. Now you're not just accumulating irritation, you're accumulating stress. You can build emotional storage accounts about people, work, problems — anything. Transforming stress involves recognizing and clearing old emotional accounts so they don't keep triggering the same old emotional habits and drains.

Breaking the Stress Habit

Emotional accounts store energy from previous reactions. They are structured by beliefs, attachments, and identities. These are often handed down from family, religion, or culture. This isn't wrong or bad. Again, these hand-me-downs are part of being human. But as human beings, we can no longer afford to remain victims of them. For the first time in history, the boundaries between different cultures are breaking down through globalization. Beliefs we grew up with, beliefs that shape our sense of who we are or what we can accomplish, are being shaken. People all over the world are going through the same types of insecurities, and at an accelerated pace. Our thoughts and ideas may differ, but our feelings are the same. It's in our *feelings* where our common humanity lives — and where our stress lives. It's in harnessing the power of our feelings that hope for the future resides.

So let's address it. In your notebook, list two or more areas where you have stored emotional accounts with another person or about work, a social issue, or a personal problem. Next, list two or more of your emotional reaction habits: for example, quick to anger when someone critiques you; always blaming yourself when something goes wrong at home; constantly judging your child, spouse, or coworkers when they don't do what you'd prefer; or blaming a different race, religion, or culture for societal problems.

Now ask yourself if there is any correlation between your two lists. What might be your underlying belief, attachment, or identity? Is it a hand-me-down from your family or culture? Note your feelings as you complete this exercise. Do you feel a sense of fear or insecurity? Do you feel a sense of release that comes from new perception or insight? Whether you feel incomplete or feel release, you can see how your emotional accounts trigger automatic reactions.

As you learn and practice the techniques in this book, you'll create the coherence you need to clear emotional accounts, and you'll free a tremendous amount of emotional energy. As you build up your emotional energy reserves and stop emotional drains, clearing old accounts will get easier. You'll develop emotional resilience that helps prevent future stress. You'll find a deeper kind of care that's perhaps different from the way you have been caring for yourself and other people. An easier and more effective care. Care that brings quicker recovery from setbacks. Care that brings empowerment, the power of your self. Care that allows you to find what your heart really wants. Care that connects you to the hearts of others. With this type of care, you give yourself sustainable emotional energy and deeper intelligence. You give yourself back your authentic self.

chapter 3

The Energetic Field of Stress

Many people write to us about stress in their lives. In addition to detailing the personal stresses they feel, their letters often convey a sense of living in a palpable atmosphere of stress, like a toxic cloud that envelops them and those around them. Today, we are all affected by an environment of stress.

An Electromagnetic Field Effect

How is an environment of stress created? It comes from the stressful emotions people feel and how these emotions are transmitted to others. A measurable electromagnetic field surrounds each person. It is a combination of the electromagnetic fields generated by the heart, the brain, and other electrical systems in the body. The heart's electromagnetic field is by far the most powerful. The heart's electrical field has forty to sixty times more amplitude than that of the brain, while the heart's magnetic field is approximately five thousand times stronger than the field produced by the brain (McCraty 2004). Researchers have found the heart transmits information via its pulsating electromagnetic field, just like cell

phones and radio stations transmit information via electromagnetic fields.

Your Emotional State Transmits

The heart pulses out a rhythmic pattern that reflects the
emotions you are feeling. If you are feeling frustration or anxiety, your heart pulses an incoherent rhythmic pattern. If
you're feeling appreciation or care, your heart pulses a more
coherent rhythmic pattern. So your emotional state is being
broadcast to your environment and to the people around you.
They are receiving your emotional state, and you are picking
up the emotional states of others, whether you realize it or
not. In fact, researchers have been able to measure one person's heart rhythm pattern in the brain wave pattern of
another person standing nearby (McCraty, Atkinson, et al.
1998; McCraty 2002). While the brain's electromagnetic field
extends just a few inches from the brain, the heart's field has
been measured as far as ten feet away, and it likely extends
much further. This means that you can be strongly affected
by electromagnetic energies emanating from someone else's
heart.

Positive emotional states that you receive from others
can give you a boost. Remember a time when you—and perhaps everyone in the room—felt uplifted by a speaker
expressing love and care. Or remember the warm glow you
felt at a birthday party when everyone was appreciating the
birthday boy or girl. Or how about a sporting event where
strangers were having fun together and you could feel the
camaraderie. Or the expressions of care between people pass-
ing out blankets to the homeless or cleaning up a neighbor-
hood after a disaster. These are examples of what a positive
heart field environment feels like. In today's world, uplifting
emotional experiences are few and far between. Negative
electromagnetic field environments are predominant. There

are understandable reasons for this. It's important not to look for who's to blame, but to understand how you can help to change it.

Amplified Speed: The Stresses of Your Daily Life

Time and events have sped up dramatically over the past twenty years due to high-speed technologies and communication systems — and people's emotional reactions have sped up with them. Fears and anxieties are amplified as a result, and so are irritations and anger. Your mind races to keep up with the onslaught of incoming information. Instant media coverage of every negative event happening everywhere raises fear and anxiety levels. On top of that, a culture of speed pushes you to multitask, doing two, three, or four things at the same time. If you don't take time to rebalance before the next task or the next download of information, your energy starts to drain. Emotions go on overload when you can't keep up with the increased pace of life. The mind's tendency is to stay glued to the Internet or incoming e-mails (even when they're not a priority) instead of stepping back to ask, *Do I really want or need to be doing this now?* So things that are more important don't get done or get done in a rush, which adds to feeling overloaded and pressed for time. You can become addicted to the stimulating pace of incoming information and demands, and get pulled along by their momentum.

> *Alicia, age twenty-two, tells of a miscommunication that resulted in her cell phone service being cut off. "The situation involved an unexpected change in the service package, and without realizing it, I incurred a monthly bill of $800. The cell phone service provider maintained their position, and until the bill was paid,*

*my service was discontinued." Alicia says she averages
1,000 minutes of cell phone use each month. This is
over sixteen hours of communication, most of it in
calls of less than ten minutes. "Without my cell
phone, I found my life changed suddenly and
dramatically. I felt like I was back in the dark ages.
My life seemed so slow! By having to rely on my
home phone line, I found I was spending more time at
home and planning things further in advance. It was
almost like a vacation, but at the same time, I was
urgently finding ways to raise the needed funds to
'get back to normal' as soon as possible."*

*Even though Alicia was able to feel more on top
of things with her life slowed down, she couldn't wait
to get back on the speedway of her "normal" life. Not
only can speed become addictive, so can doing many
things at once.*

Attention Deficit

We are bringing up an entire generation who can nim-
bly move their minds between computer, pager, cell phone,
homework, and dinner *at the same time.* But if the mind
strengthens without the heart strengthening with it, emotions
can get left in the dust. Stress abounds, and eventually the
mind becomes less effective, the feeling heart shuts down,
and the body loses out as well. Too much multitasking results
in fragmented attention and mental gridlock. It creates an
attention deficit cuture that smothers the heart and dimin-
ishes creativity. More complex emotional problems are being
experienced by children from preschool through college. It
used to be mostly peer problems, and now it's generalized
stress and anxiety. When the body has to keep working
despite mental or emotional overload, it churns out stress

hormones that can lead to memory loss, anxiety, sleeplessness, and depression.

E-mail and instant messaging major contributors to the
prevailing speed and resulting stress. Knowledge workers in
the new economy spend not only their workday checking
e-mail constantly, but considerable time at home doing the
same thing. Do you ever find yourself emotionally reacting
to just the name of the sender on an unopened e-mail, dreading what this person has to say? Each moment of annoyance,
dread, or irritation releases stress hormones into your body.
Do you find yourself checking e-mail frequently "just in
case" something important or interesting has arrived? As a
result, how many unimportant lines of communication do
you get into? And how often do you get so distracted that
you don't even realize what's happened until you're far from
your original course? E-mail eats time that you could use for
something else—perhaps physical exercise or meaningful
conversations with family and friends. It takes energy to deal
with each distraction, and when there is emotional content to
your reactions, it drains even more energy. Jim, a senior
executive, commented, "My brain needs
disk-defragmentation software, like my computer, but there
isn't any." In fact, your heart can provide that software, but
you have to give it the time of day to listen to it—at least a
little time each day.

When the mind dominates your perception and life
looks like a constant series of scheduled tasks, the heart can't
get in. The mind likes everything convenient and immediately available so it can pursue more of what it wants. The
mind can get so spoiled with technological conveniences that
if one *in*convenience gets in its way, it throws a tantrum.
How many people fret or get angry over "wasting time" trying to get information on a slow computer, when ten years
ago the same task would have required days of research and
phone calls or a trip to a library?

The speeding up of time has resulted in unnecessary emotional reactivity, mental overload, and overproduction of stress hormones. This creates a deficit of coherence, harmony, and fulfillment, because there isn't enough heart brought in to balance the mind.

The Emotional Virus

During breaks from the mundane work of our daily lives, around the watercooler or over lunch, the conversation often goes to emotional venting about "them." This "them" usually refers to the company, the boss, the management, uncooperative kids, your ex and his new family, the government—whatever or whoever you feel victimized by and lack control over. "They" are stressing you, and therefore you have a right to blame "them." One person's negativity inflames another's, and pretty soon you have an *emotional virus* spreading to all within earshot.

An emotional virus gets transmitted from person to person, group to group, through words and energies. Judgments, blame, anger, negative humor, or self-pity act as carrier waves of the emotional virus. If you're around this kind of negativity a lot, you can end up fuming, ready to incite a riot. But more likely you end up miserable and weary. You've taken on the emotional states of those around you. Your heart and brain pick up the energy like a radio receiver. One person's incoherent heart rhythm pattern, which reflects their negative emotion, gets broadcast like a radio wave through their electromagnetic field into the surrounding environment. No wonder people tend to automatically withdraw and put a protective shield around themselves in a crowded elevator.

The body easily picks up on another's feelings through a kind of emotional telepathy, whether or not the mind is conscious of it. This explains why you can feel totally drained after a meeting, even when the topic discussed wasn't particularly important to you. It's the incoherent emotional energy of the group causing your stress and fatigue. Your body feels the incoherence and produces stress hormones in response.

Susceptibility

You are more susceptible to an emotional virus when you are feeling stressed or overwhelmed. At those times, it's so easy to get sucked into others' negative emotional reactivity that your heart rhythms stay disordered and your system stays in chaos, and it's easier for a virus of any type to get in. Many people find they get sick within a few days after a binge of anger or emotional upset. When you are emotionally run-down, it's easier to catch colds or flu or develop problems in a weak or susceptible area (Cohen, Tyrrell, and Smith 1991; Kiecolt-Glaser et al. 1996). By contrast, when you are managing your emotions and your systems are functioning in greater coherence, your immune system is strengthened and more able to ward off infection and disease (Rein, Atkinson, and McCraty 1995; McCraty et al. 1996). When you're in a heart-coherent state, it helps protect you against other people's incoherent energies. This doesn't make you insensitive to others. Rather, increasing coherence gives you more compassion for their feelings and a more objective understanding of how to respond from an emotionally mature state of mind. It's no different than how a calm and emotionally steady parent has more understanding of how to help a stressed-out child than a parent who is upset or easily gets sucked into the child's antics.

Stress Is a Systems Issue

People are so interconnected that stress has become a systems issue, personally and collectively, yet as a society, we are not dealing with it on a systems level. This is because *emotions manage people more than people manage their emotions.* Our interconnectedness means we can no longer just ignore other people's stress and incoherent emotional energy. Nor can we attempt to control it by totalitarian rules. Emotions can be suppressed, but they don't go away.

Therapists report that they are seeing increasing numbers of people with mild or low-grade depression from ongoing stress. People are tired, worn out, and resigned to the idea that nothing will get better. All the negative information on TV and the dissatisfaction in their own lives makes them feel hopeless. They believe that people won't or can't change, that their job can't change, that they can't change. So why try to change anything? They've dated, had other jobs, "been there, done that," so no use trying again—it won't be any different. Saying, "I can't change" or "My life will never change" is really saying, "I won't take responsibility."

The lack of understanding of how to address emotions is the primary cause of today's stress epidemic. People generally believe that the mind is in control, but in fact it's the emotions that shape thoughts, choices, and behaviors. It's emotions that perpetuate fear and doubt. Now, just in time, scientific research has revealed that the heart can be engaged to manage emotions and provide the new perceptions needed to transform stress, both individually and globally.

Taking Responsibility

It's each person's job to ward off the stress epidemic. It's your job to do what you can to change the environment of stress. Even one person managing emotions through the heart can help change the surrounding environment. *You* can create a more coherent environment—changing what you can and cushioning what you can't—through the power of your heart's energetic expression. This takes a little practice, but so does learning to eat with chopsticks. Then it becomes fun.

It's through the heart that people change. People intuitively know this, but haven't quite discovered how to do it because they don't understand how this really works. They see examples in caring and inspiring teachers or mentors who've turned around a troubled child, and they feel moved. They watch movies based on real-life stories of ordinary people whose heartfelt courage saved a life or helped the downtrodden, and it touches their hearts. They call them heroes, and they are. Huge letters painted inside a heart on the wall of a building across from the devastated World Trade Center in New York told visitors of the power of the heart and human spirit to overcome.

Perhaps, like most people, you know all this is true, yet you still try to resolve stressful issues from your analytical mind. Without the heart, you will rarely succeed. Perhaps you engage in a sort of mental swordfight with others or within yourself while your mind searches for solutions. The mind tends to fight against stress or get resigned to it. This leads to emotional drain, because it cuts off a part of your heart in the process. As parts of the heart shut down, it changes the feelings you can experience and also narrows your perception in communications with others. Feelings become numb, dry, depressed. Perceptions become pessimistic, cynical. That's what happens in relationships when stressful issues are not resolved. Eventually, they can cause anxiety disorders, depression, or a low-grade unhappiness. You say you're happy and life is okay, but something's missing in quality and fulfillment. That something is your heart. Since the heart is your source of vitality and insight, it's important that you learn how to protect yourself from a stressful atmosphere without shutting off your heart sensitivities.

Ask yourself how the speeding up of time and events affects you. Is there a particular environment of stress that's affecting you? Have you caught an emotional virus? At home? At work? In groups or causes you are involved with? From the media? From other places? Now ask your heart what you could do to help relieve the stress. Write down your answers in your notebook.

Going Deep in the Heart

As stress continues to proliferate, more people will come to realize that they have to roll up their sleeves at times and go deep in the heart to bring about their own fulfillment. Often, when stress takes you under to a certain level, the upside is you are thrown deeper into your heart because there's nowhere else to go. And more times than not, you'll find a major release or come out with a more regenerative way to look at life.

If you're ready to finally do something about your stress, you've probably realized that there is nothing to do but take responsibility. You probably are listening to your heart more, whether or not you have called it that. Perhaps it's your heart that led you to read this book. We have found that a lot of coaching on stress relief revolves around helping people listen to and honor their heart. This often seems too easy or too simple to those who have had to strain to succeed in life (and that's most of us). The idea of loving, appreciating, allowing, supporting, and having compassion for yourself runs counter to the "no pain, no gain" model—that is, until the pain outweighs the gain. Using the heart to help clear the emotional energy field can help you see with more commonsense intelligence.

People practicing HeartMath techniques learn how to use the energy of emotions instead of feeling repressed and stressed by emotions. They learn that HeartMath practice is simple, and it works. It's like a recipe. If you use HeartMath techniques three times a day for five minutes at a time, or ten times a day for one minute at a time, you will increase your coherence and manage your emotions better. You will see and feel the impact in yourself and on those around you. If you keep it up, you will see significant changes within a couple of weeks. It starts with you.

In the next chapter, we'll turn to effective, easy-to-learn HeartMath tools for shifting your emotional state and releasing stress in your workplace, your home, your personal life, and with your children. We begin with the simplest technique, Quick Coherence, which you can use anytime, anywhere.

chapter 4

Quick Coherence

Remember the last time you felt uplifted doing something you loved, or played a great game of tennis or golf and felt "in the zone"? Getting into heart rhythm coherence takes you into the "zone."

Coherence is an important concept in high-performance physiology. In general use, "coherence" means clarity of thought, emotional balance, and the quality of being orderly, consistent, and intelligible (for example, a coherent conversation). In physics, "coherence" describes an ordered distribution of energy in a waveform (such as a sine wave). "Coherence" also means synchronization of the energy in two or more waveforms, which results in more power (for example, lasers), and synchronized interactions among multiple systems (McCraty and Atkinson 2003). Simply put, when your heart rhythm pattern is in a coherent mode, all the above definitions of coherence apply. It's that powerful.

The Quick Coherence Technique

The heart is a primary generator of rhythm in your body, influencing brain processes that control your nervous system, cognitive function, and emotion. Quick Coherence, a powerful technique for refocusing emotion, connects you with your energetic heart zone to help you release stress, balance your emotions, and feel better fast. Once you've learned the technique, it only takes a minute to do. Practicing Quick Coherence will help you find a feeling of ease and inner harmony that will be reflected in your heart rhythms. More coherent heart rhythms facilitate brain function, allowing you more access to your own higher intelligence, so that you can improve your focus, creativity, intuition, and high-level decision making. Here's how it works.

Quick Coherence Technique

1. *Heart Focus*
   Focus your attention in the area of your heart. If this sounds confusing, try this: Focus on your right big toe and wiggle it. Now focus on your right elbow. Now gently focus in the center of your chest, the area of your heart. (Most people think the heart is on the left side of the chest, but it's really closer to the center, behind the breastbone.) If you like, you can put your hand over your heart to help. If your mind wanders, just keep shifting your attention back to the area of your heart. Now you're ready for the next step, Heart Breathing.

2. *Heart Breathing*
   As you focus on the area of your heart, imagine your breath is flowing in and out through that area. This helps your mind and energy to stay focused in the heart area and your respiration and heart rhythms to synchronize. Breathe slowly and gently in through your heart (to a count of five or six) and slowly and easily out through your heart (to a count of five or six). Do this until your breathing feels smooth and balanced, not forced. You may discover that it's easier to find a slow and easy rhythm by counting "one thousand, two

thousand," rather than "one, two." Continue to breathe with ease until you find a natural inner rhythm that feels good to you.

3. *Heart Feeling*
Continue to breathe through the area of your heart. As you do so, recall a positive feeling, a time when you felt good inside, and try to reexperience it. This could be a feeling of appreciation or care toward a special person or a pet, a place you enjoy, or an activity that was fun. Allow yourself to feel this good feeling of appreciation or care. If you can't feel anything, it's okay; just try to find a sincere attitude of appreciation or care. Once you've found a positive feeling or attitude, you can sustain it by continuing your Heart Focus, Heart Breathing, and Heart Feeling. It's that simple.

In summary, to do Quick Coherence, focus your attention in the area of your heart, imagine you are breathing slowly and gently through your heart to a count of five or six, and then—while continuing to breathe with ease and rhythm through your heart—reexperience a positive feeling or attitude like care, compassion, or appreciation.

The three steps together take only a minute. That's it—one minute to transform your life in that moment, which can help make your next moments a whole lot better.

The Quick Coherence technique is very simple, but each step is important. Heart Focus shifts your energies away from the brain or mind and allows you to tune instead in to your heart. Heart Breathing shifts your system into increasing coherence, because the rhythm of your breath modulates the rhythm of your heart. This is why it's calming to breathe slowly and deeply when you're stressed: a new breathing rhythm changes the heart's rhythm, which in turn has a powerful soothing effect on the brain and the entire body. Breathing at a rate of five or six breaths per minute helps synchronize the nervous system.

Heart Feeling helps you sustain coherence without having to remain focused on your breathing rhythm. Many people find that when they experience positive feelings like care, love, or appreciation while breathing through the heart area, they immediately feel uplifted and regenerated. Sustaining a positive feeling makes it easier to sustain coherence for longer periods of time, so that it becomes natural and familiar to your system. This makes it much easier to remain calm and balanced in challenging times. Unlike meditation, yoga, and other stress reduction methods that may take time or be difficult for some people to do, Quick Coherence is a technique anyone can learn to reduce stress right in the moment, as it occurs. If it's hard for you to recall a positive feeling in the moment, take the time now to remember a couple of times when you felt uplifting feelings. Write those experiences down or memorize them, so they are easy to recall when you practice Quick Coherence.

Using Quick Coherence

Use Quick Coherence any time you want to

- increase emotional balance or improve mental clarity

- relieve worry, fatigue, or tension

- change your energetic field

- ward off an emotional virus

- help change the energetic field environment around you

- take a short break and recharge your energy reserves

You can apply this one-minute technique first thing in the morning, before or during phone calls or meetings, in the middle of a difficult conversation, when you feel overloaded or pressed for time, or any time you simply want to practice increasing your coherence. You can also use Quick Coherence whenever you need more coordination, speed, and fluidity in your reactions. Two of the top fifty PGA teachers told us how a pro they coach used Quick Coherence on the golf course as part of his preshot and postshot routines and shot his best game ever. Other golfers have lowered their score after using it just a few times. Like any form of exercise, it takes regular practice to instate a new physiological rhythm of coherence. As Harald Striepe, chief technology officer at Quantum Intech, likes to say, "Doing HeartMath is like doing crunches for your stomach muscles. You do a hundred a day, and you will see more muscle in a week. Even if you only practice Quick Coherence five times a day — that's five one-minute sessions — you will start to see results." Create an easy practice routine with Quick Coherence, and do it earnestly and genuinely.

> *Scott called to tell us he'd finally had enough and how Quick Coherence saved him. "I was on overload so much of the time that I was waking up depressed at the thought of another day of the same thing. I learned Quick Coherence from my coach and decided to use it as soon as I opened my eyes in the morning to see if it would make a difference. Using it first thing in the morning changed my attitude and perspective for the entire day. Now I use it all the time — to stop my impatience and frustration in traffic, to calm myself before talking to my teenage son and my boss, when the guy who works in the cubicle next to me starts griping and complaining, and especially when I'm overloaded."*

Deciding to Use Your Heart Intelligence

Getting overwhelmed and run-down too many times or having the bottom fall out in some area of life is what finally sends most people to their heart, screaming, *Enough, something's got to give!* They start to reevaluate what's important. They decide it's time to do something to improve their quality of life: engage in meaningful activities, start a new career, or make time count. You might ask if this is true now for you or friends you know.

Have you changed your work hours or career? Do you go to as many social events? Have you asked family or friends to expect less of you during holidays and other times that used to be filled with obligations? Do you tend to just want to stay home more or limit the number of people you socialize with? Do you want interactions that are less superficial or less negative, clearing the way for a deeper heart connection with people? Are you trying not to feel resigned to the idea that things just are the way they are? Are you actively seeking more authentic or heartfelt communication? If you have answered yes to any of these questions, then you have been reevaluating your life, and it's time to use your heart intelligence to find your next steps.

Once you've developed your skill at Quick Coherence, you will find that your heart intuitively senses more appropriate actions and decisions. We call this "heart intelligence" because it combines your brain's higher-intelligence functions with your heart skills. As you practice the Quick Coherence technique, you will be able to hear your heart's intelligence more often and more keenly, guiding your feelings with intuition and offering common sense in your thoughts. Listening to your heart is a first step; following your heart is the next. It takes courage, because you are heading into unknown territory. You'll build that courage as you see how using your heart intelligence to be more honest about feelings and more authentic in your communications really can work out.

Christine felt obligated to throw a large birthday party for a friend because it was a tradition that had been in place between them for years. "A whole circle of friends and acquaintances had built our events into their social calendars. My life had been on full tilt, and I found myself dreading the party a month before it was scheduled to occur. When someone suggested that perhaps I didn't really have to give the party, I instantly ruled it out as impossible. However, the idea took root, and after taking it to heart in some sincere self-reflection, I realized a sense of great relief in choosing not to give the party. So I spoke with my friend for whom the party was intended, and as it turned out, she was delighted at the prospect of breaking the tradition for both of us. We agreed to have a small dinner gathering with just a few close friends, and we simply let the rest go."

Obstacles to Coherence

One of the major contributors to ongoing incoherence in people's lives is that they expect themselves to do it all, then they judge themselves for not living up to their own expectations and for not being satisfied. They may know they do this and get mad at themselves for it, but they can't seem to stop. Or they assume that other people expect them to be a certain way—and maybe they do. If this describes you, you have plenty of company. The difference between people who are satisfied and successful and those who are not is the size of the gap between what their heart really knows and what they actually do. When you don't act on what you know, it's easy to fall into blame and disappointment. Quick Coherence can help you build a bridge across that gap. Each time you practice, you build more coherence and security to do what your heart knows, even if it goes against the tide of what others expect.

The stress that comes from comparing yourself to what you believe others expect of you — and beating up on yourself when you fail to meet those expectations — is often more debilitating than the stressful situation itself. You have to keep up with it all, or you feel you're not good enough. It's very common these days for people to talk about their stress levels in the way they talk about the weather, since stress is a shared experience and we're all in it together. What many don't realize is how talking about their stress can feel like they're doing something about it, when really they're *deferring* doing what they know they need to do. What stops them is a belief that they can't change without sacrificing something they don't want to give up. Their sense of self-worth is wrapped up in their stressful lives. Practicing Quick Coherence will help you see new ways through this standard human predicament, using your heart intelligence.

Letting Go of Resignation

You may be feeling that your situation is different, that there really is no way out. This is called *resignation.* There is always an opportunity to transform the stress level in any situation, if you care to. The problem is that many people feel they've cared too much, because their care has brought them more worry and stress. So they stop caring out of resignation. Caring that is stressful is *overcare.* Your attachments and expectations create overcare, and resignation comes from the disappointment and emotional drain you feel when your care turns to anxiety or isn't appreciated. You need a tool to cut through overcare and regenerate emotionally so you can bring your care back into balance. You can use Quick

Coherence to help you find *balanced care,* so you know where to draw the line and when to stop. This will start to refill your emotional reserves. And you can do it in the moment when you start to feel resigned that "she's just that way" or "it's just the way things are." One attitude shift in that moment can show you new options.

Making New Choices

Practicing Quick Coherence regularly will help you take a more honest look at your stress relief efforts and give you more objectivity and empowerment to make new choices. Go through the three steps of Quick Coherence to get your system more in sync, then ask yourself the following questions and listen to your heart for answers. Keep practicing Heart Focus, Heart Breathing, and Heart Feeling as you answer the questions. While you might not get clarity just yet, you'll start to develop *heart sensing,* or intuitive heart intelligence, as you practice. The Freeze-Frame technique in chapter 9 will build on what you learn here and help you with decision making.

 Are there activities you could modify or things you could do less of to have less stress? What would that do to your sense of self-worth? What would other people say? What would be balanced care instead of overcare?

Do you go to the gym, take walks, get a massage, take a hot bath, or do other things to relieve stress, only to find that the stress comes right back? Do you watch TV or do other activities in the name of relaxing without feeling renewed as a result? What could you do that would relax and renew you?

Have you studied or applied some type of exercise program, self-help approach, or spiritual practice? Do you try your best and feel that you're failing anyway? Does this make you feel hopeless or judge yourself? What can you do differently?

Many people have developed coping mechanisms that work to some degree, but often they give only a temporary sense of relief or escape. Wouldn't it be great to find a more solid solution? You can follow your heart to do more things that you really want to do that would be emotionally regenerative. And emotional regeneration helps prevent stress from getting to you or piling up. Use Quick Coherence to learn what your heart really wants.

 Read through the following list, asking yourself if these are things that would give you more satisfaction and fulfillment. Notice your feelings as you read through the list.

- read or write
- engage in a particular hobby
- spend time outdoors
- sleep more
- play with your children
- travel or take more vacations
- change careers or start a business
- other things you would like to do

Changing the Inside

Often, when we scan our lives to find out what's missing, we avoid looking into the stress patterns we carry inside us, like automatic judgments and blame. We try to change external things. This is like rearranging the furniture without cleaning the room. There's no true external fix for internal problems, though you can push the problem around with a temporary fix. That's like squeezing a balloon to get the air out of one end, but the air is still there, and it will push right back or pop out somewhere else. You have to deal with the underlying pattern, or it will express itself through a different problem or crisis. This can leave you mystified as to why life feels so dry, or it can send you on a wild-goose chase to find the missing factors for your peace and fulfillment.

Let's take Amelia, who wrote, 'Although my life was good, I was sad, depressed, confused, and had so many other feelings of defeat. I could not truly enjoy my life, my daughter, or my fiancé. I was so beaten down by the stresses I had endured that I could not feel the good in life. I felt like it was only a matter of time before everything came crumbling down. Now, though, since I've started practicing how to get into heart rhythm coherence, I am no longer a victim! I have learned how to hear my heart and made some changes inside that are changing things on the outside. Wow! Talk about a miracle. It's not like a magic pill that makes it all better all at once. It ignites a magic flame inside of me — the more I look at it, the stronger it gets. And the most wonderful thing about it is it's mine. No one but me truly controls it. I save energy and have stopped running myself ragged. The wonderful mother, wife, and person that I have always wanted to be, I am now! My appreciation of life and my experience sometimes grows into a huge flame that surrounds me. I could go on and on about HeartMath. It is something every person needs. It is truly the greatest gift of information I have ever received.'

Another way to change yourself on the inside is to look at how you can save energy. Ask yourself: Are you choosing more often to save your energy for what you feel you *have* to do? Still, does what you have to do drain you? Do you let yourself get overloaded and drain energy working too many hours? Do you really *need* to work that many hours, or do you just think you do? Are you refusing to take breaks or take vacations to renew your energy because you assume you'll be judged at work? Are you exhausting yourself taking care of your family—chauffeuring kids to and from activities, caring for elderly parents, doing more than your fair share of household chores, being a perfectionist in household matters, and so on?

Learning to get closer to your heart and connecting with how you really feel about the way you spend your time and energy will help you change from the inside out. Just considering these questions from a coherent perspective will start to renew your hope and your energy. You will get heart-intelligent guidance as to what changes you can make that will start to clear the air inside you. At least you will get to a more neutral state. From neutral, you gain more objectivity. You need heart coherence in your emotional system to access a clear awareness. You can't change everything overnight, but as you make even one change, other things tend to get better, and then it's easier to make the next change. The more heart coherence and positive attitudes you develop, the more you tap intuitive feelings and ideas that really are solutions. It's like tuning your inner radio to a different station by listening to your heart.

Listening to Your Heart

People naturally try to go to the heart when they're having a tough time or have a big decision to make. They may take a walk on the beach or in the woods to try to feel their heart and find some answers. Quick Coherence is a one-minute way to tune in to your heart's signals and get clearer intuition.

Remember that sincere positive feelings, like appreciation and compassion, create coherent heart signals that help open up perception and intuition. Intuition brings clarity of thought and a warm sense of knowing. It's a feeling of *Aha! Now I see what to do!* You know it's solid when you act on the intuition and things get better. You listen to your heart signals and then use intuitive perception for direction. Intuition often comes as just a simple, commonsense attitude or idea. You might not follow it because it seems too simple. But usually, simple is the solution at that moment. Act on that, and the complexities often sort themselves out later.

> Brad says, "After I use a HeartMath tool, my intuition often says, It's no big deal or Just let it go. I've intuited that before, but my mind never believed it and would keep rehashing the problem looking for a 'real' solution. With Quick Coherence, my mind is able to listen to what my heart is saying and believe it. I guess that's what the synchronization does. Things do work out, and solutions come clear later."

The mind likes to look for complexity, which is why it perpetuates so much stress. Heart intelligence looks for simplicity and ease. The mind is not the bad guy. The head and heart both do fantastic—but different—jobs. When you're analyzing or gathering facts, you use your head. But when you want to transform your stress and find more fulfillment in life, you need to listen first to your heart. The mind, in alignment with the heart, can then provide intuitive perceptions and ideas.

Practicing Quick Coherence several times a day will train you to make inner adjustments fast and develop the intuitive perceptions you need to make better choices. Each time you listen to your heart, you'll recharge your emotional energy reserves and build new confidence in yourself.

chapter 5

Transforming the Stress Response

Most of us have familiar stress symptoms we've become habituated to. Together, they make up your stress index. It's important to identify your stress symptoms so you can see where you need to use Quick Coherence and develop your heart intelligence.

 Do any of the following apply to you?

Irritability. Is your fuse shorter than it used to be? Do you find yourself getting angry at little things more often?

Loss of sense of humor. Do you find yourself feeling weighted down or too serious? Do you laugh less than you used to? Do you feel depressed or resigned to life not changing?

Worry. Do you find yourself caught in distressing thought loops, replaying anxious emotional experiences or projecting anxious situations in the future?

Excessiveness. Do you eat, drink, or use mood-altering stimulants excessively? Do you rely on stress to keep you going?

Forgetfulness. Do you find yourself forgetting little things more often? Do you feel a kind of mental gridlock?

Aches and pains. Do you have recurring headaches, frequent gastrointestinal distress, or tension in your face, jaw, shoulders, back, or chest?

Nervousness. Do you talk fast or excessively? Do you spill things more, feel more uncoordinated, have more nervous tension, or have nervous tics or other nervous symptoms?

Fatigue. Do you feel run-down a lot? Are you tired but unable to really get restful sleep? Do you have a hard time falling asleep or wake up early in the morning and have trouble falling back to sleep?

Illness. Have you been sick with allergies, colds, or flu more often? Or do you have a chronic problem your doctor has told you is stress related because no pill or other remedy has helped?

If you answered yes to three or more of the above questions, then you are experiencing some degree of chronic stress. But don't worry. Read on, because there are practical solutions you can use to free yourself from many of these symptoms.

Most of us want some inner peace and want to feel better. So why aren't we doing more to change? We asked Stan, a manager of an insurance company, that question. He answered, "Maybe we're too stressed out to do something different. We live on a stress merry-

go-round and can't get off. We think it's black or
white: quit or keep on as we are. We can't see a
solution, or if we do, we don't have the energy — or
maybe the courage — to act on it."

The Stress Habit

There is a physiological reason for not doing something different. Stress inhibits cortical function. When stress becomes a
habit, it forms a mental block that prevents you from thinking of or acting on real solutions. And so the grind goes on.
Millions of people work harder to make more money to buy
and do more things in order to make themselves happier. All
the while, health-care costs are eating away their income,
their kids are getting more stressed, and they think they have
to keep going, going, going in order to survive. And yet,
many secretly feel there must be another way. They experiment with different fixes, but mainly they just keep going.
Their stress has become a habit — mentally, emotionally, and
physically.

Your neural circuitry is exquisitely designed to form
habits to make it easier for you to perform tasks without
having to think much about them. Each time you repeat a
habit, whether an attitude, a behavior, or a repetitive task
like driving your car, it becomes more ingrained and unconscious. The same is true of the habit of stress.

Stress causes arteries to constrict, leading to high blood
pressure, which in turn can create cracks in the arterial walls
where fatty deposits become stuck and accumulate. Stress
can also cause blood platelets to clump together, leading to
clotting, which can trigger a heart attack. Depression can
contribute to heart disease for the same reasons: increased
stress hormones lead to platelet clotting and high blood pressure. People with stress-induced high blood pressure are six
times more likely to have a heart attack or other coronary

event than people with other risk factors, including smoking, high cholesterol, or diabetes (Becker et al. 2003).

Letting go of a stress habit requires changing your response to stress and modifying the information going through your body's circuitry. It helps to understand how this works.

The Autonomic Nervous System

Your brain is designed to interpret stress as a threat to your safety and security. Its stress response mechanism activates your autonomic nervous system and hormonal system for what's called "fight-or-flight" — either conquer the danger or get away fast. This ancient survival mechanism was critical when human beings had to protect themselves from wild animals and marauders. Most of our stresses today are not life threatening, yet the body's stress response system does not accurately discern the degree of threat. We react to daily stress as if it is a matter of survival, and the accumulation of these reactions takes a toll on the body. Stress is so high in some people that the response is not "fight or flight" but "fright." Fear paralyzes you, making you unable to act or make a decision.

The challenge and opportunity is to learn how to interact with your stress circuitry to regulate its response systems so they work for you rather than against you. This starts with regulating your *autonomic nervous system* (ANS), which was once thought difficult if not impossible to do. "Autonomic" means acting involuntarily; an autonomic process is one that goes on below your conscious awareness. The ANS manages a vast array of bodily processes you don't have to consciously control, such as breathing, heart rate, and digestive processes. In fact, the ANS regulates 90 percent of the body's functions.

One of the functions of the ANS is to respond quickly to a perceived threat, whether real or imagined. Think about the last time you narrowly avoided an accident. You perceived, rightly or wrongly, that another driver was about to hit your car. What happened to your body? Your breathing? Your heart rate? Your muscles? All your systems geared up to react fast. While you're busy reacting, it's difficult if not impossible to think about anything other than the threatening situation. The stress response inhibits your higher brain processes so your body focuses only on survival. When your body is responding to a perceived threat, you can't engage effectively in the kind of thinking required to plan a project or consider how you're going to handle a problem at home or at work.

The same response happens in your ANS, but to a lesser degree, when you get a voice mail or see an e-mail in your in-box from someone who has given you a tough time. You react, and your brain triggers the stress response on the assumption that the message will be detrimental to your peace of mind. When that same reaction happens dozens of times each day, your ANS stays in overactive mode, your higher brain processes shut down, and you wonder why you're overwhelmed or in mental gridlock.

The autonomic nervous system includes two branches. One is the *sympathetic nervous system,* which prepares the body for action by speeding up the heart rate. It can be compared to the gas pedal in a car. The other branch, the *parasympathetic nervous system,* can be compared to the brake pedal, because it slows the heart rate.

Emotions like frustration, anger, anxiety, or worry can cause the signals going down the two branches of the ANS to get out of sync with each other. This is like driving with one foot on the car's gas pedal (the sympathetic nervous system) and the other on the brake (the parasympathetic nervous system) at the same time—it creates a herky-jerky ride and burns more gas. Just as this causes extra wear and tear on the car, having the two branches of the ANS out of sync causes extra stress in your body.

Anger and anxiety cause activity in the sympathetic system to increase and activity in the parasympathetic system to decrease. If you are angry or anxious a lot of the time, an imbalance develops in the ANS. Since the ANS controls many bodily functions, it's easy to understand how prolonged imbalances in the ANS can lead to health problems.

What Does the ANS Have to Do with the Heart?

The brain communicates with the heart through the ANS. The activity in the two branches of your autonomic nervous system create changes in your heart's rhythms, which are measured as heart rate variability. Low heart rate variability, meaning your heart rate isn't varying much between beats, is a risk factor for arrhythmias and sudden cardiac death (Singer and Ori 1995; Vybiral and Glaeser 1995). Low heart rate variability has also been correlated with cancer, chronic fatigue, and diabetes (Bellavere 1995; Dekker et al. 1997; McCraty, Lanson, and Atkinson 1997).

A 2004 study by Duke University Medical Center researcher Simon Bacon and his colleagues found that the cumulative effect of the daily mental and emotional stresses of life lowers the amount of heart rate variability, which reduces the heart's ability to respond appropriately to the outside world. Using monitors that measured participants' heart rate variability twenty-four hours a day during everyday life, the researchers found that higher levels of negative emotions were strongly associated with a reduction in the ability of the heart to respond to stress. Negative emotions like anger or sadness corresponded to lowered heart rate variability, reflecting a reduction in autonomic control of the heart. Bacon commented, "Sick hearts show very little heart rate variability, so they are not as responsive, leaving them vulnerable. Healthy hearts have a better ability to respond to anything that occurs. The bottom line is that the stress we experience throughout the course of the day can be bad for our hearts" (Merritt 2004). It's important to understand that your heart rhythms can be in coherence with low or high heart rate variability. In addition, we have found that when people with low heart rate variability practice managing their emotions and sustaining heart rhythm coherence, their overall heart rate variability is increased.

Your Brain Listens to Your Heart

Your heart rhythm pattern is affected by more than your autonomic nervous system. It's also affected by your heart's intrinsic nervous system, or the "brain in the heart," which receives hormonal, emotional, and other information from the rest of your body. Amazingly, this "brain" in the heart senses, feels, remembers, and communicates that information to the brain upstairs.

Your heart communicates with your brain in four important ways: *neurologically* (through the nervous system), *biochemically* (through hormones and neurochemicals produced within the heart), *mechanically* (through the pulse wave flowing through the bloodstream), and *electromagnetically* (through electrical signals generated when the heart contracts and broadcasted through the heart's electromagnetic field) (McCraty and Atkinson 2003).

To help you understand the heart's role in stress, we'll focus on the neurological communication between the heart and brain. The brain relies on neurological information from the heart. In fact, the heart sends more signals (more neural information) to the brain than the brain sends to the heart (Armour 2003). Your heart rhythm pattern tells the brain what the body feels, and your brain then interprets the information and decides what to do. The heart communicates information by way of the *vagus nerve* to the thalamus and the amygdala, both key centers in your brain.

The *thalamus* is designed to distribute incoming information to the appropriate brain centers and to synchronize cortical activity. Incoherent heart rhythms inhibit cortical function; coherent heart rhythms facilitate cortical function and higher reasoning (McCraty 2003; McCraty and Atkinson 2003).

The *amygdala* is where emotional memories are processed. The amygdala compares input from the heart and the senses—sight, hearing, touch, smell, and taste—with information stored in your emotional memory banks. The amygdala scans for patterns that match what it's experienced before. When the amygdala receives a heart rhythm pattern or sensory input that it associates with a past experience, it detects a pattern match. In fact, the cells in the core of the amygdala synchronize to the heartbeat (Frysinger and Harper 1990). If the past experience was stressful, the amygdala triggers the stress response and the negative emotions associated with that experience. The reason you react negatively to a name appearing in your e-mail in-box is that your amygdala has stored unpleasant memories of that person.

Emotional Assessment Tracks

There are two tracks by which the brain makes emotional assessments from input it receives. The *slow track* goes from the thalamus to the cortex and then to the amygdala. The *fast track* goes from the thalamus directly to the amygdala, bypassing the cortex.

The cortex is the conscious, decision-making area of your brain. It taps into your beliefs and attitudes to decide what to do. But before it has time to consider all the factors to determine an appropriate response, the information traveling on the fast track can reach the amygdala first. If that information resembles a negative emotional experience from the past, it can trigger a reaction that seems irrational when considered objectively. It's irrational precisely because the information traveled on the fast track, which bypasses the rational part of the brain.

Suppose that a man is walking down the street and sees a puppy. The thalamus sends the image of the puppy directly to the amygdala; it also sends the image of the puppy to the cortex. The amygdala searches for an emotional memory match and recalls when, as a young boy, the man was bitten by a dog. Before the cortex can decide that it's just a harmless puppy, the amygdala can trigger a fear reaction similar to the one the man had as a boy when he was bitten or just a feeling that he doesn't like dogs even though he doesn't remember why.

Stress habits develop in the same way. Stress behaviors get deposited in the emotional memory banks and create emotional accounts that affect how you perceive and react to situations in the present. Fast-track responses can create strong reactions or lead you to behave in ways you later regret. With hindsight, you wonder why you said something inappropriate or why you reacted a certain way. By intervening in the fast track, you can transform those automatic stress responses.

Transforming the Stress Response

People need stress-relief measures that have more long-range effectiveness. They need tools that relieve stress on the spot or prevent stress before it triggers them. Too often, people try a binge-purge approach to stress relief. You get stressed out and wait for the "cure" to change how you feel—a massage at the spa, a game of golf, a trip to the gym, a shopping trip with friends, or a long-awaited vacation. As good as these activities may feel, they won't change your stress habits. And a majority of people in the world don't even have access to these stress relief options. Managing your emotions *when you experience stress,* rather than after the fact, is what transforms your habitual stress response.

A study published in 2003 by University of Wisconsin neuroscientist Richard Davidson and colleagues found that certain meditation techniques can change the stress circuitry when practiced over time. Techniques that help you detach momentarily and get a new perception are the key. As a new pattern becomes ingrained through practice, new pathways are formed in the cortex.

Most cognitive behavioral therapy methods try to help people change their perceptions and responses through the slow track. But the fast-track triggering of old memories and emotional reactions can override and undermine cognitive efforts. So what is needed is a fast-track approach to managing and relieving stress that clears the emotional memory banks.

By using HeartMath techniques, you change your heart rhythm and emotional or attitudinal state, right in the moment when you're perceiving and feeling stress. This changes the signals going from the heart to the thalamus and amygdala, and you've broken the stress habit in that moment. With practice, new habits are built that transform the old stress circuitry.

Why Changing Your Heart Rhythms Is More Effective

Changing your heart rhythms, as you do with techniques like Quick Coherence, is more effective at relieving stress than techniques like relaxation. If you're feeling worried, frustrated, anxious, or angry, relaxation can turn down the volume on this emotional noise, but it doesn't change your stress circuitry. Shifting your heart rhythms and emotional state is how you change the fundamental patterns of your stress habit. Your heart is designed with the key systems to help you do just that.

Look at it this way. Relaxation is a parasympathetic response (the brake). When you have deadlines to meet or need to get a task done quickly and efficiently, relaxed isn't necessarily the best state. You need sympathetic activity (the gas) to get up and go, which is why people think they need stress to stay motivated. But to perform at your best, you need to be both energized and at ease. You need both branches of the ANS to be in sync, working together in harmony.

Managing emotions and heart rhythms is a choice you make to free yourself from the stress response trap. It's a choice of intelligence to go to your heart and select appropriate emotional responses that bring new perceptions. Heart intelligence can help you decide whether a traffic jam is a huge, inexcusable inconvenience that enrages you or just a minor event that is beyond your control and might even be a gift of time in which to slow down and plan your day. You have the choice to invest your emotional energy in reactions or to self-regulate—and that choice makes the difference between empowerment and victimization.

> As Kathy, a HeartMath client, says, "Being able to feel the difference in my body with HeartMath tools made me want to maintain it all the time. When I first started, it reminded me of the movie Hook, where Peter Pan needs to feel a happy thought in order to fly again. I'd gotten so wrapped up in my everyday stresses, and even stresses that hadn't happened yet, that I needed to learn how to 'fly' again by feeling positive emotions and changing my stress responses."

Finding the Courage to Change

Many of our clients, especially corporate managers, have been taught that the heart is "soft" and in business you should rely on your head instead. In fact, the opposite is true. Your heart is your main source of strength and power. The heart is not where you become trapped by your emotions; rather, it is the source of your power to transform them. Going to the heart to manage your emotions and get clear perceptions is what your body is designed to do. Going to the head and reacting is easier, because it's what people automatically do. It takes courage to take emotions to the heart and use techniques for self-regulation. And it's something you have to choose to do. It takes courage to manage your emotions from your heart's intelligence, because it's easier to let emotions follow your mind's reactions. Once intuitive guidance from the heart is accessed, then your mind and emotions come into more alignment with the heart. User-friendly tools are needed to facilitate the alignment between heart, mind, and emotions. You advance at the speed of your commitment to practice. Commitment comes easier as you see progress in the energy you save from emotional drain.

The word "courage" is from the Latin and French derivative word for heart, *coeur*. It takes courage to be honest and admit stressful feelings like frustration, resistance, and anxiety. Courage is a quality of spirit, a mental or moral inner strength to venture and persevere to withstand fearful thoughts. To be courageous is to be vulnerable, in touch with what you are feeling, while having the strength to go back to your heart and not succumb to the stress response. Bruce Wilson, cardiologist and chairman of the board of the Heart Hospital of Milwaukee, says,

> *The HeartMath tools, in my opinion, are the simplest to learn and most effective methods to break stress and change the entire cascade of neurological and biochemical*

events triggered by stress. You can use HeartMath tools to help you regulate your heart rhythms to gain autonomic control, feel positive emotions, and find new perceptions. The HeartMath techniques engage the power of your heart to transform your stress. It's a choice to connect with that heart intelligence and then to act on what you see.

chapter 6

Sustaining Coherence

Once you learn how to shift into your heart coherence, the next step is to learn to sustain it for longer periods and get back to coherence faster when you're out. By sustaining coherence and getting back more quickly, before your emotional energy drains, you gain new views on old issues that have kept you down or still run you around. You want to build and sustain enough coherent heart power to rewire your stress response circuitry.

Getting Pulled Back: Anxiety and Anger

Perhaps you have new perceptions or insights on how to make things better, but you don't act on them because your stress response patterns keep pulling you back to your same old ways. You *know* better but aren't able to *do* better. Even when you have a breakthrough or get a glimmer that a situation is different than you'd believed, entrenched patterns can pull you back to old perceptions and beliefs as if you never had the insight.

> *Laci was unable to keep from venting anger and frustration with Kyle, her significant other, and knew*

she was destroying the relationship. She tried therapy, self-help workshops, and support groups, but nothing seemed to work. She would have breakthroughs, see things differently, and get excited. She'd tell Kyle, and he'd support her. But then she would fall back into old insecurities and reactions and take them out on Kyle. When he'd remind her, "We've been through this already, and I thought we got to the other side of it," she'd get angry and say he didn't care about her. Kyle felt that no matter what he said or did, Laci didn't want to hear any other viewpoint. He was tired of being a dumping ground for her emotions when she wasn't making any efforts to change them. They argued frequently. Laci was driving away the person she cared most about, and she felt powerless in the situation.

What can Laci do? She's so sure of her perceptions, and she isn't able to control her angry reactions. What can Kyle do? He watches Laci have breakthroughs and immediately revert to her previous beliefs.

Pete works as a painting contractor, spending much of his time alone. For company, he listens to talk radio. The content of the programs — as well as the hype of the ads — upsets him, and yet he believes he needs to stay informed about what's happening in the world. All day long he listens and reacts, sometimes getting angry at what he hears, sometimes getting anxious and upset. Occasionally, a particular topic will bring him to tears, and he'll find himself shouting, "Who cares?" to the blank walls. He blames others for the way things are, and he blames himself for not being able to do anything about it. The state of the world and his own sense of entrapment have left him feeling isolated and hopeless.

*How does Pete get out of this box? He's tried
turning off the radio, but he keeps turning it back on.
He knows he should find some other means of
entertaining himself during the day. Pete feels he'll be
disconnected from the world if he doesn't keep
listening. He wants to be able to listen to the news
without getting so upset, but he doesn't know how.*

*Sheila's young adult son was diagnosed with bipolar
disorder, a mood disorder which can manifest in
varying degrees of drama or violence. Her life now
revolves almost totally around this son and his
disorder, despite the fact that she is an executive with
a high level of responsibility, much of it with
international clients. Whenever her beeper goes off,
she doesn't know if it will be a customer in Asia, a
troubleshooting expert reporting from Mexico, or
someone reporting bad news about her son. She feels
tension, worry, grief, and rage by turns, all while
trying to maintain business as usual. Her son takes
medication, but she never knows when the next crisis
will occur, and she can't see any solution. Sheila
knows that she should hire someone to help but
doesn't. She keeps feeling that as a good mother, she
should do it herself. What's Sheila to do?*

Millions of people get stuck in their ways, like Laci,
Pete, and Sheila. It's not bad. It's the human condition. But to
find happiness, you need to get unstuck. Otherwise, you are
like a puppet on a string, dancing to your same old perceptions and predictable reactions. Learning to get into coherence opens up perception. Learning to sustain coherence
gives you the power to identify and break free of limiting
perceptions and beliefs.

As you can see in the previous stories, there are two
chief pathways by which people tend to get stuck in their

perceptions: the anxiety pathway and the anger pathway. Furthermore, either pathway can trigger the other, so you can end up both anxious and mad.

The Anxiety Pathway

Let's look at the anxiety pathway. Many times, when something unexpected or new occurs, it can cause a fear or insecurity. You feel afraid simply because you haven't experienced that situation before; it's a fear of the unknown. Or you have had a similar experience and have a negative coloration in your emotional memory because you haven't really understood that experience yet. So you are expecting the new situation to be as stressful as you remembered the previous one to be. This *fear projection* creates stress even though nothing has happened yet. Insecurities are at the base of fear projections — fear of personal inadequacy (of not being special, not getting approval, not being enough, or not having enough), which leads to perfectionism, guilt, unbalanced ambition, and angst-driven anxiety. Fear and anxiety exist on a continuum. They're rooted in the same physiology. Anxious people tend to continually restock their emotional accounts that contain fear projections, keeping their stress hormones busy. Anxiety takes a significant toll on the heart.

Your system can pick up fears and insecurities from people around you — or from the TV or radio, like Pete. If you don't acknowledge the feeling of insecurity and take it to your heart to find balance and coherence, you can end up feeling a low-grade anxiety without knowing why. The mind then projects fearful scenarios. This only increases the anxiety. If the anxiety isn't resolved, it builds on itself. Your system will keep producing certain neurotransmitters and hormones that keep the fear going, raising your baseline stress level.

Fear is also created from having experienced hurt and pain in the past and not wanting to experience them again. This is understandable. But you don't want that fear to perpetuate an anxiety *trait,* a habit that becomes second nature. Memories of hurt and pain can perpetuate a continuous, low-grade to extreme anxiety, causing ongoing subtle to obvious energy drains. Through practicing HeartMath techniques, you gain new wisdom from your heart intelligence that releases the anxiety. You can let that wisdom become your reference to not keep setting yourself up to repeat the same patterns that result in hurt and pain.

Cavigelli and McClintock (2003) discovered that rats that are fearful in infancy maintain this trait throughout their lives and age prematurely, often dying young. They have higher levels of the stress hormone *cortisol,* and this takes a toll on their bodies. When the rats were faced with change or novelty, cortisol levels spiked in both fearless and fearful rats but remained high in the fearful rats. Similarly, baseline levels of cortisol stay elevated in fearful children and adults. Reflecting on the results, Cavigelli concluded, "It's worth thinking about how we perceive the world and how that affects our physiology" (Simon Silver 2003).

Changing the Anxiety Trait

The good news is that studies show that people can change long-standing traits and lower their cortisol levels through the power of the heart (McCraty, Barrios-Chaplin, et al. 1998). HeartMath tools have been shown to be effective in changing stress patterns in people with congestive heart failure, diabetes, high blood pressure, and other chronic diseases (McCraty, Atkinson, and Lipsenthal 2000; McCraty, Atkinson, and Tomasino 2003; Luskin et al. 2002). Our own study with HIV positive and AIDS patients (Rozman et al 1996) showed that practicing HeartMath techniques for six months significantly reduced long-standing traits of anxiety and fear. (Improvements in trait anxiety are rare, even in healthy populations.) Participants also showed significant improvements in irritability, positive affect, physical vitality, hardy outlook, behavioral and emotional symptoms of stress, and general well-being. In addition, they reported reductions in a wide variety of pathological symptoms, including infections, anemia, herpes, and fatigue. Half of the participants who reported physical symptoms at the start of the study reported no symptoms after completion of the six-month practice program. Two of the participants were able to discontinue certain medications with their physicians' approval by the end of the study. Participants experienced changes in perception, feeling, attitude, and behavior more profound than they had previously achieved through years of various treatment programs, support groups, and individual psychological counseling.

> *D. M., a participant in that study, wrote, "My arrival at HeartMath was accompanied by a hopelessness that had consumed my soul. I had been diagnosed HIV positive and felt sentenced to a meaningless death. The changes in both perception and attitude since that time are numerous! I'm no longer waiting for that 'meaningless death.' Instead I have a mission, one of loving life and myself. Each day brings gifts, not despair. My life still has its stressors, but they no longer bring me down into suicidal depression. The HeartMath practices have aided me in all aspects of my life: physical, mental, and emotional."*

The most effective way our research lab has found for people to release anxiety or fear is to intentionally bring more coherence to their heart rhythms and learn to sustain coherence through shifting attitude and emotional states. You can use Quick Coherence with your feeling of anxiety or fear. To help yourself understand your anxiety or fear, identify those feelings and bring them to your heart, then befriend them by feeling compassion, care, or appreciation for yourself or something in your life. Those attitudes and positive feelings will quickly bring your heart rhythms into greater coherence. Coherence sends a different signal to the brain, opening a communication pathway between your heart and brain that will help you understand the fear and help loosen its hold on you. Then you can practice the Heart Lock-In technique, which we'll teach at the end of this chapter, to help sustain that new coherence.

The Anger Pathway

Like anxiety, anger is another pathway that can trap you in old patterns. When you feel impatient, irritated, or frustrated, it's because you perceive that something is getting in the way of what you want or how you think things should be. Something has inconvenienced you or done you wrong. These perceptions and feelings lead to judgments and blame, and often build to anger.

Justified or not, anger triggers incoherence in your heart rhythms and activates stress hormones. The stronger the anger and the more emotionally out of control you are, the more anger blocks your brain from seeing different perspectives. Anger hormones give you a quick energy burst, but incoherence will quickly drain you. If you allow an impatient or angry feeling to run this course too often, you'll end up with low-grade hostility. Hostility is a risk factor for heart disease, even for children and teenagers (Raikkonen, Matthews, and Salomon 2003). When you're angry, you see the world through defensive eyes. Something or someone is out to get you. That can convince you to go on the offensive to get them before they get you.

An anger mind-set is built from inflexible attitudes and hormonal patterns that reinforce those perceptions and feelings. Your mind gets stuck "knowing what it knows," which can maintain a slow, acidlike burn in your feeling world. You're pumping out hormones that keep your stress levels high and your stress reactions in gear. Once you've built an anger (or anxiety) mind-set based on "knowing what you know," it can be very hard to release what you believe you know or let anything new get in. Even if you get a glimpse of a new view, like Laci, your previous mental perceptions and emotional reactions can rear their heads and take over again.

Changing the Anger Pathway

You can use the same HeartMath techniques for intervening in the anger pathway as you can for the anxiety pathway. Quick Coherence (from chapter 4) and Heart Lock-In will help you shift your emotional state toward coherence and see situations around you in a new way. Remember, progress happens in ratios, as we described in chapter 2. Appreciate any progress you make. Practicing these techniques regularly will help you anchor yourself in the new perception and sustain coherence so that you don't slip back into previous views and reactions as often. Eventually, you will change the trait and be free of old habits of anxiety and anger.

Laci, Pete, and Sheila all used HeartMath techniques to change their emotional states and their traits. They saw new solutions and had enough sustained coherence to act on them. Laci was able to finally feel and understand what Kyle was trying to tell her and hold on to her new perceptions. Pete used the Heart Lock-In technique to shift his feelings and perceptions about the state of the world. He was able to send compassion and care to the situations that previously made him feel hopeless. He realized he wanted to connect with people and make meaningful contributions to his community. Sheila spent fifteen minutes a day practicing the Heart Lock-In technique to build her power to sustain coherence and listen to her heart intelligence. She achieved a more balanced care for her son and found new ease with the situation.

Realigning with Your Inner Security

Learning to listen to and follow your heart results in increased security. As your inner security increases, you become more clear and effective in stressful situations—and in creative endeavors. Building inner security is worth the effort it takes to achieve it. That's because the lack of it is the major block to manifesting the power of who you really are. In short, this entire book is about building inner security through aligning with the intelligence of your heart.

You can start increasing inner security by generating attitudes and feelings of compassion, care, appreciation, and forgiveness to engage your energetic heart. These positive emotions release different hormones, which feel better to your system. That's your body's way of saying, "Yes, feel these more." As you feel more secure, you see that you have a choice about where to keep your energy: in your head, reacting with anxiety, fear, irritation, or anger, or in your heart, to sustain coherence, security, and insight.

Try it and see what it's like to generate appreciation, love, compassion, or care from the heart. These attitudes transform stored stress and add renewal to your whole system. As you process your emotional reactions through the heart for balance, often you will find that situations aren't as difficult as you had expected. Stored-up anxieties lessen and irritation and anger are transformed as you learn to use your heart to sort life's issues.

Locking In Coherence

The Heart Lock-In technique transforms emotional traits and physiology by helping you unfold and sustain coherence. Heart Lock-In is an emotional restructuring technique that helps you instate new attitudes that are aligned with your real self. You learn to generate in yourself positive energy of appreciation, compassion, love, and care and to send or radiate that energy to yourself and to others, thus changing the energetic environment within and around you. Loving yourself and others in this way is one of the most efficient ways to transform stress in yourself, your home, and your workplace. People may not know what you are doing, but they will feel the difference in your balance and composure. They often feel better themselves as you help create a different frequency environment.

✎ *Heart Lock-In Technique*

1. Gently shift your attention to the area around your heart.

2. Shift your breathing so that you are breathing in through the heart and out through the solar plexus. (The solar plexus is located about four inches below the heart, just below the sternum, where the left and right sides of your rib cage are joined.)

3. Activate a genuine feeling of appreciation or care for someone or something in your life.

4. Make a sincere effort to sustain feelings of appreciation or care while directing them to yourself and others.

5. When you catch your mind wandering, gently focus your breathing back through the heart and solar plexus and reconnect with feelings of care or appreciation.

After you're finished, sincerely sustain your feelings of care and appreciation as long as you can. This will act as a cushion against recurring stress or anxiety.

Quick Heart Lock-In Steps

1. focus

2. appreciate

3. sustain

Practice the Heart Lock-In technique in a quiet place for five to fifteen minutes one or more times a day to build your power to sustain coherence. Some of the most effective times to practice are first thing in the morning, to start your day; at a midafternoon break, to "reboot" and reenergize your system; and before you go to bed, to promote more restful sleep. The body naturally goes into the coherent heart rhythm mode in states of deep, peaceful sleep.

If emotional histories or resistances come up while you practice, just send forgiveness, care, or compassion to these patterns to bring more coherence to them. *Resistances* are uncomfortable feelings or sensations that can have weight to them. You may not even know why the discomfort is there. That's normal, until you unlock the emotional history or fear underlying it. Befriend and send compassion to the resistance to help release the blockage. Resistant feelings come and go and are released gradually as you gain more heart intuition about them. When thoughts and concerns pull you into the head during a Heart Lock-In, bring your focus back to the heart. Keep pulling your attention back to the area around your heart and build your power to stay in your heart. Breathing into your heart and out through your solar plexus helps give you more power to anchor your attention in the heart. This helps activate intuition.

When you first start practicing Heart Lock-In, generate the feeling of appreciation or care by choosing something that's easy to appreciate, so your coherence is not compromised by unresolved emotional issues. If you can't *feel* appreciation or care, simply adopt an *attitude* of appreciation or care. It's fine to picture a person or situation, like a child, pet, or place you love, in order to establish a sincere feeling or attitude of appreciation or care. But it's important to then let the visualization go so you stay focused in your energetic heart, radiating the feeling and attitude to your body or directing it toward others.

After you practice awhile, you will open to new perceptions and creative ideas. Write down ideas you'd like to remember to put into action. Often, these will be attitudes or ideas that you already knew. You may have even had a strong intention to act on them before, but something was blocking so you couldn't follow through. The Heart Lock-In technique will help you sustain the power to carry out your good intentions. Your attitudes will shift and your inner security will build as you learn to sustain coherence.

chapter 7

Transforming Stress into High Performance

While everyone experiences stress, what you do with it makes the difference in how much happiness and contentment you experience. It also makes a difference in how you perform in your work. In this chapter, we'll show you how you can transform stress into optimal performance at work and in every area of your life.

Velma Wachter, vice president of nursing, and Mary Laubinger, director of quality management at St. John's Mercy Hospital, saw the power of sustaining coherence during a very challenging time at work. Every couple of years, all hospitals endure visits from outside auditors, and the visits are a huge source of stress. It starts with the worry and anxiety of preparing for the visit, then more stress during the visit and while waiting for the results.

"We worked many hours to prepare for the joint commission visit and consistently used the Heart Math tools," says Mary. "In the final days before the visit, we realized that everything that needed to be accomplished would not be done in time. By using the tools, we were able to achieve clarity to focus on

summarizing five projects for the document review session. As it turned out, there was just enough time to get those five projects finalized. At the end of the survey, the auditors remarked that ours were some of the best-prepared documents they had ever reviewed."

Velma adds, "We decided that during the visit, we would start each day by doing the Heart Lock-In technique. As we escorted the surveyors around the hospital, we continued to support each other in feeling appreciation and maintaining coherence. As the surveyors interviewed individual staff and inter-disciplinary teams, we weren't allowed to answer questions, but we could continue to shift to our hearts and send love and appreciation to our coworkers. This made a profound difference in shifting the initial tension and nervousness the staff experienced. The staff was able to respond beautifully to the questions. Their ability to maintain coherence was felt by those around them, and it made a difference as the survey progressed. Other leadership team members and managers commented that these surveyors were tough and expressed fear that they would have problems. We kept using the tools and responded, 'We will do fine.' When it was all over, St. John's Mercy Hospital received a score of 99 percent — quite an achievement! We attribute our success to our ongoing use of HeartMath tools that allowed us to stay centered and positive, both preparing for and during the actual survey. Our energy was preserved, and we had the clarity to handle last-minute challenges without becoming frustrated or exhausted."

HeartMath techniques, when you practice them regularly, improve your stress-to-performance ratio. You transform stressful feelings into emotional resilience and clarity to meet challenges with a positive frame of mind, as Mary and

Velma did, and improve performance as a result. You also save your energy and health.

Stress Hormones

Let's look at what happens to your body chemistry when you experience stress. A cascade of 1,400 different biochemicals is released by the body as soon as it senses stress. These hormones and neurotransmitters affect how you perceive and feel. High stress keeps your system bathed in stress hormones, which speeds up your biochemical aging clock, draining emotional buoyancy and physical vitality. Stress makes you feel like you're living to survive instead of to enjoy life. You wake up in the morning dreading the day, sure it will be no better than yesterday. Your perceptions and feelings signal your body to release stress hormones into your system, depressing your mood and decreasing your ability to face the day's challenges.

Adrenaline

The *adrenal glands,* which lie on top of the kidneys, are where the two major stress hormones, adrenaline and cortisol, are manufactured. Adrenaline is released when the sympathetic branch of your autonomic nervous system gets aroused. Adrenaline can give you a boost like a cup of coffee. Strong emotions, like anger or fear, release a lot of adrenaline into your system, but adrenaline doesn't stay in the bloodstream for long. This is why anger or fear can give you a surge of energy and a temporary high but leave you feeling drained afterward. Too much adrenaline, too many ups and downs, can lead to high blood pressure and burnout.

Steve, a company president, suffered from high blood pressure and had a short fuse when under pressure, which was a lot of the time. He snapped at people, threw papers around, and made decisions too quickly, thinking that he was just moving things along. Others complained they had to pick up after his mistakes. "I didn't think I was like that," says Steve. "After learning HeartMath tools for health reasons, I was able to see what I'd been doing. I also was able to normalize my blood pressure in just nine weeks, and it's stayed normal. I'm a better person to work for. Even my ex-wife told me I'm easier to get along with and asked what I've been doing."

Cortisol

Another important hormone related to stress is cortisol, often called "the stress hormone." While cortisol is a necessary hormone (if cortisol didn't naturally peak in the morning, you might not wake up on time for work), when you chronically produce more than you need, it can lead to a host of problems. Over time, excessive levels of cortisol can cause sleeplessness, loss of bone mass and osteoporosis, allergies, asthma, acid reflux, ulcers, low sperm count, redistribution of fat to the waist and hips, and fat buildup in the arteries, which can lead to heart disease and numerous other diseases (McCraty, Barrios-Choplin, et al. 1998). All of these are the body's efforts to protect itself.

Negative emotions fuel higher cortisol levels. This means that every time you are anxious or angry, or even rehash a stressful situation, your brain signals your adrenal glands to pump more cortisol into your system. Excessive amounts of cortisol linger in the bloodstream for hours, which can tend to increase feelings of anxiety. Too much cortisol also depresses the immune system, opening the door to infection and other diseases. Elevated cortisol levels have been shown to shrink the hippocampus, the memory-storing area of your brain (Lupien et al. 1998). When too much cortisol accumulates in the hippocampus, thinking becomes fragmented and you can't remember as well.

Catecholamines

In addition to adrenaline, stress releases other *catechol-amines* (neurotransmitters) that deactivate the *prefrontal cortex* of the brain, a higher cognitive center critical for effective concentration, planning, and decision making (Arnsten 1998). This explains why you have trouble thinking clearly when you are excessively stressed. Pressure mounts, and instead of being able to face it calmly, you find yourself getting flustered, unable to see the best course of action or even imagine a good outcome.

> *For the past several years, since her life became highly stressful, Sally has had difficulty focusing. She has to reread documents several times before she understands them, and even then, she finds it difficult to remember what was said. She tends to give up and let others make decisions at work. She struggles in deciding what to wear, what to do about problems at work, or even what to eat for dinner. Sally feels dejected and has been told she has adult attention deficit disorder, but she didn't used to have problems with concentration, planning, and decision making when her life was less stressful.*

Sally's response to stress is what's called a *defeat reaction,* while Steve's angry, impatient response is a *defense reaction.* When the body can no longer tolerate the overload imposed by stress, it undergoes more physiological changes to try to adapt to the situation, and you can end up exhausted and depressed. Cortisol secretion increases further, immune resistance breaks down, and the stage is set for disorders and accelerated aging.

> *Drew came to a HeartMath seminar in a state of exhaustion. He was forty years old but looked sixty. Drew was suffering from an autoimmune disorder, slept fitfully, and was very overweight. He told us that for years, he would eat junk food to relieve his stress, and now he wanted to learn tools to transform the stress. People always told him that fat people were happier and that he seemed happy. But he knew deep down that he just pushed feelings away and put on a mask of happiness. Many obese people he knew weren't happy and ate because they were stressed.*

Stress and Overeating

Surveys show that 46 percent of Americans are less careful about what they eat when stressed (Harris Interactive 2002). People who are stressed are also more likely to eat quickly or to binge. Chemical messengers that influence why, what, when, and how much you eat function less effectively when you're under stress, making it harder to tell when you have eaten enough (Rosch and Clark 2001). Cortisol converts fat into energy to help you respond to the stressful situation, but if your cells don't burn the energy, it gets redistributed into fatty deposits around the waist and hips.

At least 64 percent of the U.S. adult population is now overweight, and 31 percent is obese, reports the Centers for Disease Control and Prevention (Flegal et al. 2002). These numbers are on the rise and show no sign of abating. The CDC estimates that if something doesn't change drastically, the number of obese people in the United States will reach 40 percent by 2010 (International Health, Racquet & Sportsclub

Association 2004). The problem isn't limited to the United States. Around the globe, about 1.7 billion, or one in four, are now overweight, according to the International Obesity Task Force (Ross and Verrengia 2004). People's girth has grown along with their stress levels.

Feel-Good Hormones

Fortunately, there are hormones that help offset the biochemical stress response. *Dopamine* and *oxytocin* are hormones that can uplift your moods. Only recently was it discovered that these hormones are produced by the heart as well as the brain (Horackova 2004). *Dehydroepiandrosterone* (DHEA) is another feel-good hormone. Like cortisol, DHEA is produced by the adrenal glands, and it helps counter the effects of cortisol.

DHEA

DHEA has been called "the antiaging hormone" because it's plentiful in young people. When you produce large quantities of DHEA, you feel vitalized. DHEA and cortisol are made from the same precursor hormone, *pregnenolone.* So when DHEA is high, cortisol is low; at these times, you feel younger, more energetic and vital. When cortisol is high, DHEA is low; at these times, your energy is low and you may feel older than your years. In fact, one of the most accurate physiological indicators of stress and aging is the DHEA-to-cortisol ratio (Namiki 1994).

Stress and your emotional state strongly affect the ratio of cortisol to DHEA. When you're feeling stressed, your body will produce more cortisol (the stress hormone) at the expense of DHEA (the feel-good hormone). That's okay in the short term. However, consistently high cortisol combined with low DHEA has been found to be a factor in sleep disorders, obesity, diabetes, chronic fatigue, depression, migraines, fibromyalgia, osteoporosis, high cholesterol, and other chronic conditions. In fact, DHEA is low in a person with almost any major disease (Parker, Levin, and Lifrak 1985; Shealy 1995). Low DHEA and high cortisol levels equal rapid aging.

Transforming Your Hormonal Responses

Positive emotions increase production of DHEA, which promotes emotional vitality and slows aging. Learning how to shift your emotional state and attitude throughout your day improves your ratio of DHEA to cortisol. DHEA lingers in your bloodstream for a long time and helps to sustain a good mood. By lowering your cortisol and increasing DHEA levels, you strengthen your ability to face stressful situations calmly and meet challenges with a positive frame of mind.

Reducing Stress Hormones

In one study, participants using HeartMath techniques reduced their cortisol levels by an average of 23 percent and increased their DHEA levels by over 100 percent in just thirty days of practice. The participants also experienced reduced anxiety, guilt, burnout, stress, and hostility, along with increased caring, contentment, warmhearted emotions, and vigor (McCraty, Barrios-Choplin, et al. 1998).

A controlled study of employees at Unilever, a global consumer goods company, showed that those who used HeartMath techniques experienced changes in stress hormone metabolism and concurrent changes in systolic blood pressure over a six-month period. DHEA levels were increased by about 70 percent after just three months and rose 90 percent after six months. Measures of weight and abdominal fat were also improved in the group using HeartMath techniques, compared to the control group. Blood pressure reduction was significant, taking the population using the HeartMath treatment from high normal to optimal (Cobain 2002).

In both these studies, participants raised their DHEA levels without increasing exercise or taking supplements. Unless your doctor prescribes it, we do not recommend that you try to raise your DHEA levels by taking DHEA supplements, because this won't necessarily lower your cortisol levels and can cause other imbalances in the body. DHEA supplementation by women can lead to beard growth and acne. DHEA supplementation by men can promote prostate cancer. DHEA is a banned substance in the Olympics because it is a performance enhancer. And taking hormone-changing supplements doesn't change your stress perceptions or reactions. You can change your hormones naturally as you change your perceptions and reactions. Increasing DHEA and lowering cortisol through becoming more emotionally balanced and resilient is natural, safe, and long lasting, with no negative side effects.

Releasing Depression

A 2004 study sponsored by Sedona Training Associates found that 48 million Americans — or approximately one in four — have taken antidepressants such as Paxil (paroxetine), Zoloft (sertraline), or Prozac (fluoxetine). However, 57 percent report they continue to feel depression, stress, and anxiety, and those taking antidepressants are five times more likely to consider suicide. This study, which focused on Americans' attitudes toward stress, happiness, and everyday quality-of-life issues, also revealed that 44 percent of those taking antidepressants find work stressful, and Americans taking antidepressants were twice as likely as those not taking antidepressants to quit or be fired because of difficulty coping with bosses and coworkers. The study concluded that Americans are more aware of day-to-day quality-of-life issues than ever before but are still uncertain how to deal with stress and emotional turmoil (Sedona Training Associates 2004).

One of the primary reasons for these dismal statistics is that letting negative thoughts and emotions run rampant generates stress hormones which keep circulating in your system and reinforce depressed mood and anxiety. When you are in the habit of engaging in negative thought loops, fear projections, blame, and resentment, the hormones they release (and the insecurities they stimulate) will continue to run through your system even if nothing external is triggering them.

Fortunately, through increasing and sustaining coherence, you can change your autonomic nervous system response, your hormonal ratios, your moods, and your perceptions. You can not only transform stress but also increase your high-quality emotional energy that supports high performance.

You don't have to be a victim of your hormones. Rather, as you manage your emotions by using techniques like Quick Coherence and Heart Lock-In, you reengineer your biochemistry to create the physiology you need for peak performance and minimal stress. This state is characterized by a sense of security and pleasure, ranging from a relaxed sense of harmony to more intense positive emotions such as happiness, joy, and appreciation.

Improving Your
Stress-to-Performance Ratio

Figure 7.1 illustrates that emotions reflect high or low arousal of the sympathetic nervous system (high or low energy) as

Stress, Emotion, and Physiological Activation

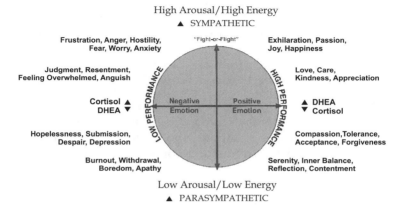

High Arousal/High Energy

▲ SYMPATHETIC

© *Copyright Institute of HeartMath*

Figure 7.1

well as the ratio of DHEA to cortisol. High-energy emotions create high arousal in your sympathetic nervous system and can be negative or positive. Some examples of negative high-energy/high-arousal emotions are strong frustration, anger, hostility, fear, worry, anxiety, judgment, resentment, anguish, and a feeling of being overwhelmed. Positive high-energy/high-arousal emotions include exhilaration, passion, joy, happiness, love, care, kindness, and appreciation. Low-energy emotions create more parasympathetic activity and can also be negative or positive. Negative low-energy/low-arousal emotions include hopelessness, submission, despair, depression, burnout, withdrawal, boredom, and apathy. Positive low-energy/ low-arousal emotions include compassion, tolerance, acceptance, forgiveness, serenity, inner balance, reflection, and contentment.

Though shifts to higher or lower levels of arousal are appropriate at different times, emotionally fit people tend to return to a positive emotional balance point between high and low arousal. Then they can carry out day-to-day activities with optimal effectiveness and peak performance.

 Consider yesterday's events. In your notebook, make a list of activities, situations, and events you experienced. Then describe your moods or emotions during each activity the best you can. Turn to the next page in your notebook and divide it into quadrants corresponding to the quadrants in figure 7.1. Place each of the moods or emotions in the appropriate quadrant. For example, a positive, high-arousal emotion like exhilaration would go in the upper right-hand quadrant. A negative, low-arousal emotion like apathy would go in the lower left-hand quadrant.

What emerges is a snapshot of the emotional landscape of your day. The right side is the high-performance zone. The left side is the low-performance or stress zone.

Once you get an idea of your day-to-day emotional landscape, you can begin to see why it affects your stress-to-performance ratio. Figure 7.2 is based on research conducted during World War II about what happens to soldiers when they are under stress. Your life environments can sometimes feel like a war zone, and your ability to perform at your best can be affected much the same way.

When you are first exposed to stress in the form of a challenge, arousal of your sympathetic nervous system increases. Your performance at first improves. This explains why many people feel that stress motivates them. Maintaining a positive attitude helps lengthen the time of maximum

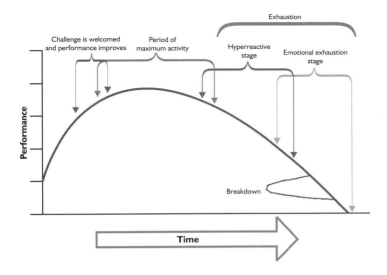

Figure 7.2

This figure has been adapted from R. L. Swank and W. E. Marchand. 1946. Combat neuroses. *Archives of Neurology and Psychiatry* 55:236–47.

efficiency. But at a certain point, as the level of challenge or amount of work increases or stays high, your ability to perform at your best is compromised. You find yourself working longer and harder just to keep up. You may also find that you're more likely to react with irritation or anger. Most people don't notice when their performance slips.

If your stress level isn't reduced, you will eventually get exhausted. The state of exhaustion results in a breakdown in your ability to function well mentally, emotionally, and physically. Some typical signs that you are on the downslope include loss of focus and mental clarity, increased negative emotion and attitude, inability to relax or sleep well, loss of self-esteem, feeling tired and on edge, and finding it a struggle to motivate yourself and others.

Where the curve peaks is different for different people depending on their *emotional resilience*. Those with more resilience perform at higher levels for longer periods. Those with less resilience reach their peak earlier, have less capacity for coping and adapting, and have greater tendencies to become exhausted and sick. However, even those with high resilience will succumb to exhaustion and illness if the challenge lasts long enough.

In many workplaces, harried employees feel they are under constant stress from too much pressure, too many meetings, too many inefficiencies, and too much to do. The environment is rife with blame and judgment. Courtesies are expressed on the outside while emotions are out of control on the inside.

While writing a book on stress and performance at work, Bruce Cryer, president and CEO of HeartMath LLC, the HeartMath training company, asked senior managers at a high-level meeting of a global telecommunications company for their assessment of the corporate culture. One exhausted manager said, "Only the dead have done enough," which was met with complete understanding by others in the room. Corporate life evokes this cynical view in many people. But such a high level of pressure actually prevents people from performing at their best. As the president of a leading advertising agency told us, "I used to measure my work productivity in a day by how stressed I felt. After learning the HeartMath techniques, I realize I get more done—and done better—when I'm not stressed."

HeartMath LLC provides performance training to executives and managers of world-class companies like Sony, Shell, Cisco, Boeing, Unilever, BP, and Liz Claiborne, using before-and-after assessments to track participants' progress. Surveys of nearly fourteen hundred employees at five global companies conducted six months after they began using HeartMath methods showed the following sustained results: 60 percent reduction in anxiety, 45 percent reduction in exhaustion, 41 percent reduction in intent to leave the job, 24 percent improvement in the ability to focus, 25 percent improvement in listening ability, and 17 percent improvement in homework conflict. Employees learned how to stop their stress reactions and improve their emotional resilience (Childre and Cryer 2000).

Many children come to school stressed from problems at home or with peers. Educators have found that children who learn HeartMath tools to release anxiety and stress — and shift their attitude and outlook — can quickly improve their test scores. Controlled studies with high school students have found improvements of 14 to 35 percent in math and reading in just three weeks (Arguelles, McCraty, and Rees 2003). Now that's resilience!

Developing Resilience

Just as you take in food and transform it into energy, you transform positive emotions into buoyancy and resilience. When you are resilient, you can get yourself started again quickly if you get stalled. Stress drains that ability by scrambling the messages going through your brain and nervous system and increasing the stress hormones coursing through your body. Without reconnecting with the heart, it's hard to find that resilience.

People who are resilient tend to regularly appreciate the good things in their life and don't make too big a deal out of problems and inconveniences. They are able to choose positive attitudes and feelings in the face of challenge, which quickly improves their biochemistry. They tend to have a healthy DHEA-to-cortisol ratio. Resilient people also tend to have a strong commitment to core heart values, a sense of control over the outcome of their life's course, and an abundance of energy, which makes it possible to enjoy the challenges of life.

Through practicing the techniques in this book, you too can increase your emotional resilience, maintaining higher performance levels as you meet the challenges of work, family, and life with increased buoyancy and equanimity.

chapter 8

The Power to Shift Attitude

We've talked about how important it is for your health and peak performance to have positive feelings and attitudes running through your system during your day. So how do you learn the skill of quick attitude shifts?

At times, it's clear when a person needs to make an attitude adjustment. Perhaps you've heard friends telling each other, "Girl, you need an attitude adjustment" when one is negative for too long, or teenagers talking in the school hallway saying, "You've got an attitude problem." Maybe you have friends who you know aren't going to see any way out of their problems until they change their attitude.

But changing an attitude can feel like an uphill struggle or a do-good attempt at positive thinking with no juice behind it. You need power to change negative momentum and make attitude shifts that you *feel* are real. So what can you do?

The Quick Coherence technique can help you shift feelings and attitudes fast. But there are times you'll need extra power to shift a negative attitude and make it stick. You can add that power with a HeartMath tool called Attitude Breathing. Attitude Breathing powers you up by getting more of your physiological systems in sync. It harnesses the power of your gut as well as your heart to take the fire out of negative emotions so they have less hold on you. With Attitude Breathing, you can change those adrenal stress hormones more quickly and find your way back faster to an attitude of calm and balance. Before we show you how to do Attitude Breathing, let's look at why it works.

The Three Brains

The functions of the brain have been categorized in three levels. The first level governs a lot of your instinctual reactions, the second level is involved in the processing of emotions and memory, and the third level adds thinking, reasoning, and the ability to project into the future and plan. As you synchronize the communication among these three brain levels with the "heart brain," you build the capacity to take more control of yourself and shift emotions and attitudes faster. Getting more of your systems in sync helps you build more staying power.

The Gut Brain

When you perceive a threat, the brain signals a system of nerves in the area of the stomach and solar plexus that is sometimes called the "gut brain." These nerves control your digestive tract, which is why you can feel butterflies in the stomach when you're anxious or afraid or a knot in the stomach when you're angry or upset (Gershon 1999). If you experience gut stress a lot, you may develop chronic abdominal upsets or irritable bowel syndrome.

The gut brain is also where you feel the instinct to take or avoid action. Have you ever heard someone say, "I just followed my gut" or "I felt it in my gut"? Many people confuse gut feelings with intuition. The gut brain is more reactive and instructive than intuitive.

The Heart Brain

The heart also has its own nervous system, the "heart brain." The heart brain takes an active role in communicating with the head brain, sending more signals to the head than it receives in return (Armour 2003). Recent studies have shown that the heart brain receives intuitive information before the head does. Scientific evidence indicates that intuitive information is received first by the heart; then it's sent to the brain (head); then the brain signals the body, which responds (McCraty, Atkinson, and Bradley 2004a, 2004b).

Getting Your Systems Synchronized

The second level of your brain, residing in the center of the brain, enables you to experience emotion and to store emotional memories. This is where the thalamus, amygdala, and hippocampus are located. The activity of the core cells of the amygdala (where emotional memories are stored) synchronizes to the heart's rhythm (Frysinger and Harper 1990). This may help explain why the heart has long been associated with the experience of feelings and emotions, and it may be why people use expressions like "warmhearted" or "heartfelt," "a heart full of joy," and "heartache" or "heartbreak." The heart is literally sending information to the second brain level about how you feel (McCraty 2003).

The third level (consisting of the cortex and neocortex) enables you to think and reason. This is where you analyze and interpret feelings, intuition, ideas, and sensory experiences. You use your third level to recognize that you're in stress, acknowledge the stress, and make a conscious choice to take a time-out, use a tool, or do something about it. When you use HeartMath tools and shift into a coherent mode, the three levels of your brain work together more harmoniously. Hindsight and foresight come together so you can make more intelligent decisions in the present. Your cognitive and emotional systems become more synchronized and aligned, which facilitates emotional clearing.

Through the practice of shifting your heart rhythms into the coherence mode, you will build power to make faster attitude shifts. As you practice sustaining the coherent mode for longer periods, it helps bring more coherence to the rhythms of the gut brain as well. Thus, with practice, not only do the three levels of your brain become more synchronized with the heart, but a systemwide level of coherence occurs where the heart, head, and gut brains all get more in sync. You need this extra coherence power to solve and clear difficult, entrenched problems. Coherence makes it easier to find a neutral state, and a higher order of objectivity can become available to you.

Attitude Breathing

Attitude Breathing is a tool that helps you synchronize the nervous system activity in your entire body—the heart brain, the three levels of your brain (head), and your gut brain. By using this tool regularly, you gradually build the power to make attitude shifts that last. Attitude Breathing will restructure your emotions and repattern your neural circuitry and hormonal responses so you can change long-standing unproductive attitudes, including those you are not even consciously aware of.

Many people have grumbles and gripes running as background noise behind their thoughts. This makes the day look bleak, like a black-and-white movie, instead of colorful, vibrant, and filled with rich texture. Attitude Breathing will help you clear out these old gripes and negative undercurrents so you can minimize the stress hormones running through your system and gain access to the feel-good hormones that keep you feeling vibrant.

✏ *Attitude Breathing Tool*

1. Focus on the heart as you breathe in (as you learned to do in the Quick Coherence technique). As you breathe out, focus on your solar plexus.

2. Practice breathing in through the heart and out through the solar plexus for thirty seconds or longer to help anchor your energy and attention there. Next, select a positive feeling or attitude (try appreciation, for example) to breathe in through the heart and out through the solar plexus for another thirty seconds (or longer).

3. Once you feel the appreciation, lock in the *feeling* of that positive attitude. Now, as you breathe, visualize building and storing the positive energy that the feeling of appreciation gives you. Practice breathing that appreciation for a few minutes.

4. Select attitudes to breathe that will help offset the negative emotion or imbalance of the situation you are in. Breathe deeply, with the intent of shifting to the feeling of that attitude. You can breathe two attitudes, if you'd like. For example, you can breathe in an attitude of balance and breathe out an attitude of forgiveness, or you can breathe in an attitude of love and breathe out an attitude of compassion.

Using Attitude Breathing

Practice different attitudes you want to develop. You can tell yourself, "Breathe courage," "Breathe ease," "Breathe forgiveness," "Breathe neutral," or whatever attitude you need. Even if you can't *feel* the attitude shift at first, making a genuine and earnest effort to shift will at least help you get to a neutral state. In neutral, you have more objectivity and you save energy.

Attitude Breathing is especially handy during highly charged situations. The tool combines the power of the heart and gut to enable you to shift emotion and physiology right in the middle of a strong reaction. The heart is the most powerful rhythmic oscillator in the body, so it pulls the body's other rhythms into synchronization with its own. Your power to make attitude adjustments will build fast as you use Attitude Breathing in the middle of a reaction or disagreement.

When you first try Attitude Breathing in a charged situation, it can feel like you're going against the grain or against what you know about the situation. You may have to apply earnest effort against resistance. During strong reactions, you may need to breathe the new attitude earnestly for two or three minutes before your nerves quiet down and you experience a shift. Do it for the sake of creating coherence. Do it for yourself. Have a genuine "I mean business" attitude to really move those emotions into a more coherent state and shift your physiology.

 Use your notebook to write down unproductive attitudes you know you have and more positive attitudes you wish you had. Now think of that nemesis in your life or that person who gets your goat or has been a problem for you. Consider what attitudes might help you stay in more coherence when you're around (or even when you think of) that person. Pick one or two and use them in Attitude Breathing.

Simply focus in the area of your heart while breathing those feelings or attitudes. Try attitudes opposite from what you've been feeling—for example, love and appreciation if you've been feeling animosity and resentment. Breathe the feelings of love and appreciation in through the heart as best you can, then breathe them out through the solar plexus area. Imagine love and appreciation flowing in and out with your breath until you find an easy rhythm with it. Don't worry about whether you are doing it right. Just look for the rhythm. Practice this genuinely and earnestly for thirty seconds or longer. Then stop and note what you perceive and feel. The shift might be subtle, but you will probably be more balanced about the situation.

Attitude Breathing in Daily Life

It's fun to experiment with different attitudes. You will develop new awareness of what each attitude feels like and what it can do for you. Practice Attitude Breathing until you remember to do it automatically when you feel irritated, frustrated, angry, anxious, or fearful. These emotions speed up the aging process. This tool is a countermeasure against unhappiness and aging.

Use Attitude Breathing several times during the day— *even when nothing is disturbing you*—in order to build up a storage bank of positive emotional energy. When you're feeling great, breathe joy or appreciation and store that positive energy. The advantage of stored positive energy is that it helps lift you above frustrations, anxieties, and gridlocks in day-to-day life that would otherwise drain you. It gives you a chance to sort out challenges without them taking you down. When these stressors still take you off guard, reboot your heart power by taking a moment to go back to Attitude Breathing.

Attitude Breathing works on the same principle as putting money in the bank. It's handy in times of need. The idea is to build a cushion or reserve you can draw on when negative situations start to sap your energy. You can breathe any attitude that's appropriate for the situation. For example, when you find yourself reacting to a stressful situation, try breathing the attitude of emotional calm. This is important because on the other side of calm are the energetic storms that emotionally drain you. Remembering to practice Attitude Breathing while in the midst of stress often stops the draining process and especially helps you replenish energy after you're already drained. With practice, Attitude Breathing stops payment on energy drains before stress issues pull you into their negative loops and exhaust your emotional accounts.

Most energy drains happen when you get sucked into others' downward spirals. When your positive-attitude energy is drained, it leaves you operating on nerve energy without emotional salve, which increases the stress in your physical system. Earnest practice of Attitude Breathing can change this. But remember, it's important to do Attitude Breathing from your genuine heart, because if you do it just from the mind—without the heart—you won't draw enough power to shift. Positive thinking alone is not enough to shift attitudes highly charged with emotion. Adding heart power is the missing factor, because it puts spirit behind intent.

Attitude Breathing can help you plan ahead for situations you expect will be stressful and leave you more prepared to handle the unexpected. Try breathing attitudes of taking significance out, nonjudgment, balance, emotional calm, alignment, compassion, forgiveness, and other attitudes that instill emotional strength. Breathing these attitudes stores positive energy to be used when you need it.

Let's say tomorrow you're going to a meeting, and you know that some of the items on the agenda are going to bring up stress and frustration. With Attitude Breathing, you can start today and power up enough emotional strength to breeze through the meeting without becoming another victim of the storm. In this type of situation, you can breathe the attitudes of balance and emotional calm. Of course, these attitudes are not just for meetings. They can prepare you for any encounters with children, spouse, certain people, issues, or situations that you already know are loaded with potential for stress.

Remember, it's not so much *situations* that drain you. It's the amount of repetitive negative thought and *emotional significance* you assign to those situations that depletes energy. *Practice taking significance out of anything.* You can do that by breathing the attitude of taking significance out. This is one of the most important attitudes that you can breathe. Attitude Breathing to take significance out strengthens your power to make effective changes in your day-to-day world and in your life in general.

Emotional preparation before any predictable stressful scenario can save tons of energy in a day, and even more over the course of a week or longer. The energy you save improves your health, stockpiles happiness, and slows down the emotional aging process. This is something we've proved in the HeartMath labs. Emotional drains accelerate aging and sap vitality. Attitude Breathing is a serious and effective tool for preventing that.

Learn to practice Attitude Breathing while you're taking a walk, exercising, driving, walking to and from the office—anywhere. Post reminders to do it on your bathroom mirror or computer, PDA, or cell phone. Practicing will store strength and flex in your emotional nature. The energy saved is internalized and used by your body for healing old patterns in your mental, emotional, and physical self. It moves old emotional patterns out and replaces them with positive strength patterns that become hardwired in your system as you practice.

 One of the most effective times to practice Attitude Breathing is during the first thirty minutes after you wake up in the morning. Play an Attitude Breathing game. Start attitude breathing as soon as you get out of bed, and see how long you can continue to do it.

Breathe appreciation or balance, for example, while you're taking a shower, getting dressed, making breakfast, getting the kids off to school, and so forth. Especially breathe balance and emotional calm when things are running late or there are traffic gridlocks while you're driving to work. Practice the tool casually as you go about your business. When you get distracted, just remember to go back and practice Attitude Breathing instead of processing all the negative stuff that can come up in the morning. Make it into a fun game, and it will set a different tone for your day. Our research at HeartMath has shown that this tool alone helps to provide an emotional cushion through daily stressors. It helps to prevent your emotions from becoming frayed and causing you to then have to operate on nerve energy— producing drain.

When you don't want to practice, when you'd rather hold on to a reaction or pout, or when a negative reaction "owns" you, go against the grain of habit and generate an attitude shift. Each time you do this, you'll progress in transforming your nervous system and hormonal responses.

Ann, an elementary school teacher, was reassigned to a junior high class due to a teacher shortage. She found the kids testy and daunting. Ann says, "Each morning I'd wake with a sense of dread, not wanting to face the day. And once I woke up, it was hard to shut my mind off. I would worry, blame myself for my shortcomings, or be thinking of how I could do things better. When I faced the first class, I was still fighting the anxiety, not knowing what back talk I was going to get from these kids today. After I learned the heart–solar plexus breathing, I used it each morning. I did it while getting dressed and ready for the day, in spite of the fact that anxiety was causing

*my solar plexus to churn and my mind was racing. I
also did it in spite of the fact that I could not feel
my heart. I just kept telling myself to breathe ease
and appreciation for the kids I liked. By the time I
sat down for my morning coffee, I could feel a shift.
Sometimes it would be to a more calm and centered
place. At other times, a warm feeling of love would
flood into my heart, or a sense of peace. No matter
how agitated I felt upon rising, by really going for
the Attitude Breathing, by the time I faced my
students, the sense of anxiety and dread had eased
and I felt ready to face the day. I also have found it
valuable to remind myself to do Attitude Breathing
during the day, and it's helped me maintain inner
security and balance. It has not been an easy teaching
year, but without the Attitude Breathing tool, I can't
imagine what this year would have been like."*

Attitude Breathing on the Job

At work, people sometimes communicate poorly, and
feelings can get hurt. Once emotions are bruised, people easily slip into judgmental reactions, which are downshifts
toward negativity and incoherence. If you lose a lot of
energy when your feelings get hurt, your energetic field
turns negative, and you are likely to pass that negativity on
to others.

Through genuine heart effort, you can interrupt the
cycle with Attitude Breathing. Shifting to a positive attitude
helps you cut your losses and release the accumulated stress.
Don't underestimate what you can do when your heart is
behind the doing.

Attitude Breathing helps keep emotional energy
grounded in highly stressful job situations. Emergency workers learn to do it (often unconsciously) because they must.

They have to shift out of emotional reactions quickly, or the stress would block their ability to make fast, effective, life-saving decisions and lead to burnout. They develop the capacity to focus their energies in the heart and solar plexus to balance their reactions to life-and-death situations.

> *Solano, an ER assistant, told us that when he first learned Attitude Breathing at a HeartMath training at his hospital, he realized it's what he does automatically when a patient is brought into the trauma room.*
> *Solano says, "I was so glad to see there's a scientific reason behind what I was doing and why it works for me. I didn't even know that's what I was doing until I did the Attitude Breathing in the workshop. I always breathe in care and compassion through my heart to get myself right and then anchor that feeling in my solar plexus to stay grounded and not overreact to the situation. I still react some, but it takes the extra emotion out. It keeps me centered to see how best to treat the injury — and the person, too."*

Other Important Times to Use Attitude Breathing

Here are some other ways you can use Attitude Breathing.

When you have difficult conversations with children, spouse, relatives, or friends. Use Attitude Breathing before (if you can), during, and after the conversation to stay in your heart and keep yourself as balanced and secure as possible.

When you can't sleep because your thoughts are racing. Use Attitude Breathing for five minutes to clear the slate.

When you wake up feeling anxious about your day. Use Attitude Breathing to restart your day and reboot your system. Make a commitment in your heart to start each day fresh.

When fear projections surface about what might happen today or tomorrow. Use Attitude Breathing for a few minutes to center yourself and prepare for whatever might happen next. It could be better than you think.

When you find yourself ruminating with a negative attitude. Tell yourself, "No, stop, don't go there. I've been there, done that, and I know where it will lead." Use Attitude Breathing with the intent of restructuring that pattern and stopping the energy drain.

When traumatic memories resurface. Use Attitude Breathing for a few moments to interrupt the neural pattern. Regular practice of Quick Coherence, Heart Lock-In, and Attitude Breathing will lessen the impact of traumatic memories and, over time, help repattern the neural imprint. Many people with post-traumatic stress disorder report that their attacks become fewer and less severe when they practice these HeartMath tools alone or as an adjunct to other therapies.

Don't Postpone Positive Change

It's easy to put off looking at certain attitudes and emotional habits in yourself, but putting it off only makes other aspects of your life worse. If you put it off because you think it's no big deal or because you're afraid to look, you are denying what your heart knows really needs to be addressed.

When you defer emotional responsibilities, such as shifting negative attitudes, it's like accumulating credit card debt that you'll have to pay later. On an energy level, it really does work this way. Your negative attitude drains you emotionally, and you go about your business with grumbles, gripes, and fatigue going on underneath. It's all you can do to keep up with paying the interest on what you're deferring. You can't get ahead because you're always behind. Every time you get one thing cleared, two more problems to gripe about pop up. Eventually the debt grows to the point that it's all you can do to make the minimum payment each month.

Building power to make attitude adjustments reverses your emotional debt. Interest compounds in your favor, like it does in a savings account. What you appreciate appreciates in value, just as a savings account appreciates in value.

Instead of wasting your energy in deferred feelings, use that same energy to make attitude shifts. Be glad to know *whatever* you are feeling, because now you have tools and techniques to redirect your energy wisely. As you use your energetic heart intent to generate attitude shifts in yourself, you'll change your internal pharmacy (your hormones and biochemistry) and experience more buoyancy, freedom, and a sense of youthful energy. This is an antiaging formula.

Change Is an Act of Integrity

Knowing you need to shift an attitude and deciding to make the change is an act of integrity you owe to yourself. Holding to a new attitude even when it takes your feelings awhile to clear is also an act of integrity. As you grow in integrity, you become more secure and solid in your real self. Your own commonsense heart intelligence will guide you. You'll find you are moving through life in a new rhythm that's much more fun and effective.

chapter 9

Going Deeper in the Heart: Unraveling the Mysteries of Life

Transforming stress in individuals and society requires an emotional shift, not just a mental shift. Over the past hundred years, humans have undergone rapid development of the mind on a global level. Billions of us now are connected by television, Internet, and cell phone—our ideas and inventions cross all borders. People think the mind runs the world, but emotions do more so, and emotions often defy logic and reason. Technological advances in the hands of the emotionally irresponsible can cause global and economic chaos. As human beings, we are at a juncture where we can't keep advancing mentally and ignore emotions, because emotions won't ignore us.

Managing and Clearing Emotions

What we need now is rapid development of the ability to understand feelings and to manage and clear emotions. Emotions create structures that influence how people think and behave. These structures might include old stress accounts left over from mistreatment by a relative or coworker. They might be cultural or religious accounts handed down from parent to child over decades or centuries. They might be old grudges held on to because of fixed attitudes. Whatever the source of these accounts, they are made up of old emotions that haven't been cleared. If these emotions aren't released, the future will look a lot like the past: dominated by greed, fear, and revenge.

On an individual level, emotions are the key to happiness. Many therapists are beginning to realize that therapeutic approaches that do not focus on emotional shifts (such as cognitive behavioral therapies that rely on reason and logic) simply do not bring about effective change. A 2004 *Washington Post* article reported that approaches that appeal principally to logic and reason often fail (Morse 2004). As a result, more therapists are training patients to get in touch with their feelings, attending to the knot in the stomach or the pain in the heart. That connection allows deeper feelings to emerge. Then the therapist trains the patient to self-soothe to shift emotional state. Morse quotes Chicago area therapist Brent Atkinson, who says, "Unfortunately, the more logical and intelligent clients are, the more they think they can do it without practice."

Emotional Agendas

On an interpersonal level, conflicting emotional agendas often prevent people from solving problems effectively. For example, when engineers working on a construction project hit a snag, they come together and figure out a solution to the problem—unless emotions like jealousy, resentment, or vanity define the agenda and undermine their efforts. As anyone who works in universities, businesses, governments, or politics knows, fair and effective decision making is often hampered when people pursue emotional agendas. These create stress and incoherence that prevent people from seeing or doing what would be more effective. Emotional agendas are often unconscious, based on insecurities or beliefs about how things should be. Our emotions are trying to sell us (and often others) on something, whether a perception, an attitude, or a belief.

Emotional agendas create unconscious stress patterns that keep people stuck. That's why even smart people who really want to manage their emotions often can't change. Change requires some emotional reengineering, and this involves the heart.

Emotional Reengineering

We use the term "emotional reengineering" because anything less just won't solve the problem. When people try to shift a negative attitude or emotion, they often try to *act* as if the problem weren't there, or they try to shift into *thinking* positively. But with these methods, they aren't able to build up enough coherence to clear the underlying emotional belief. It takes a coherent heart intention to get down to business about things that really count, to shift emotional physiology and clear agendas and stress accounts that regulate your quality of life. It takes the power of heart intent to reengineer emotional responses to bring happiness with minimal stress.

Accumulating Stress Accounts

You make deposits in your stress accounts by storing unresolved feelings of stress. Remember that feelings are information that's trying to tell you something. Feelings aren't bad or wrong. But they can seem that way when you don't understand them. Everyone experiences stress feelings at times. We all have felt scared, blamed, sad, lonely, worried, insecure, anxious, fearful, edgy, reactive, irritated, angry, bored, moody, hurt, jealous, guilty, pouting, greedy, envious, constricted, repressed, resentful.

Most everyone knows how it *feels* to grieve, to feel boxed in, to be numbed by hurt and disappointment, to be emotionally weakened and fatigued, to feel resigned and hopeless or overwhelmed. Stress builds up also when you feel that things aren't fair, feel misunderstood, feel unappreciated, feel unnoticed, feel inadequate or inferior to others, or feel superior to others. Many people feel these emotions and attitudes recycling beneath their thoughts through much of the day without being resolved, and they drain energy.

Soothing or uplifting feelings are also felt by all: care, kindness, warmth, strength, love, appreciation, compassion, hope, forgiveness, peace, joy, and bliss. You can probably add others to this list. These generate increased coherence in the human system and add to your energy.

All human beings want to feel more soothing or uplifting heart feelings and less of the stressful feelings. Studies show that happiness is not based on money or material goods, as long as people have adequate food, shelter, and warmth (Baker and Smith 2003). Yes, money and conveniences are nice add-ons, but they can't be depended on for your primary peace. Happiness has to do with the amount and duration of positive heart feelings people experience. Those who feel a deep spiritual connection or have close bonds of heart and friendship with family and community report being the happiest, whether they are rich or poor, American or Nigerian. By the same token, stress has to do with the amount and duration of incoherent feelings we experience and store in stress accounts.

 Take another look at the list of stress feelings above. You may think of others to add to this list. Write down in your notebook how often you experience each of the feelings: hourly, daily, weekly, not often, or never. Then do the same for the list of soothing or uplifting feelings to get a picture of your happiness.

What Happens When You Don't Clear Feelings?

To relieve stress in yourself, you have to help relieve it in others, since their stress affects you, too. There can't be stress relief for one person or group at the expense of another, as this only perpetuates the endless cycles of stress, separation, retribution, and even violence. Often, people don't have a clue what others really are feeling. That includes people with whom they work or live. Much of the time, people don't know what they themselves are feeling or know how to express a feeling in a way that others will hear. Most people's emotional difficulties come from not knowing how to clear feelings as they arise. So they stay inflamed with emotions that accumulate in stress accounts.

Gary describes how this happens in his relationship with his wife. "I get so pissed when Jenna and I argue and don't stop and talk about it. All day I'm ruminating about what I should have said or done. Then I get extra angry or hurt because Jenna won't call me to try to clear it up. I know I could call her, and I even call myself stubborn for not making the phone call myself to try to clear the issue. This happens over and over." Gary knows exactly what needs to happen: one of them needs to make the phone call to reestablish communication. Gary recognizes that he is being stubborn when he refuses to make that call. He needs a good dose of heart

*intention to muster the courage to take the first step
toward Jenna.*

Clearing Stress Accounts

It takes *heart vulnerability*—admitting your deeper feelings—to
face the fear and make the call. Heart vulnerability is not emotional vulnerability, where you get caught up in and cave in to
your emotional state. It's just an honest admittance from the
heart of what you are feeling. Heart vulnerability can seem
hard at first, because the mind anticipates that it will create
more pain or loss. Gary is afraid that Jenna is still angry and
won't hear him. Maybe she will even blow up at him. But
when you are vulnerable and admit your deeper feelings, it
tends to open others' hearts, and negative outcomes are less
likely. It helps you clear as you go.

Heart Vulnerability

Heart vulnerability releases tension and helps you create a more coherent waveform in yourself as you connect
more deeply with your heart. Going deeper into the heart
allows intuition to surface and shows you easier ways to feel
about things. Being heart vulnerable helps liberate you from
fear or insecurity as you listen and communicate your real
feelings. Heart vulnerability reveals your underlying emotional agendas or beliefs that may be blocking you. And it
opens your heart to hear the feelings of another as well as
your own. That's why heart vulnerability is a coherence-building power tool.

In the lab, when we measure heart rate variability in
people who are quietly inflamed with internal resentments,
we see that their heart rhythm pattern is very jagged, disordered, and disturbed. As soon as we coach them to use

techniques like Quick Coherence, Attitude Breathing, Heart Lock-In, or Freeze-Frame (which we'll teach later in this chapter), they establish a new inner rhythm. In this more coherent rhythm, they begin to get in touch with deeper feelings. They become more heart vulnerable and thus more honest with themselves and other people about what they are feeling.

When you can't get past the hurdle of fear and be heart vulnerable with yourself or another, be as easy on yourself as you can and find compassion for yourself. Use the Quick Coherence technique to go deeper in the heart. Use the Heart Lock-In technique and send yourself compassion, understanding that your fear is shared by others and is very human. Ask your heart to help you take a next step with compassion. Compassion is an attitude or feeling that brings in more heart coherence and eventually more clarity.

Heart Vulnerability Activates the Energetic Heart

Heart vulnerability activates the energetic heart so you can finally clear emotions at their source, then regrid emotional patterns and attitudes. Remember, it's the stored emotions that feed overdrive, anxieties, and angst—that feed stress. Learning to tune in to and operate more from the energetic heart is what draws intuitive guidance to clear old stress patterns and prevent new ones from forming. It's from the energetic heart that you get the emotional salve to move through stressful situations without getting as caught up in them.

The term "energetic heart" can sound complex, yet you can make it simple by remembering that it's the place people tell each other to go when they say, "Speak from your heart," "Play from your heart," "Be genuine," or "Be grateful." It's a feeling and attitude that goes with the place they are referring to. This place is what connects you with your heart intelligence and helps to prevent cumulative stress and to clear patterns of stress already accumulated. That's what the HeartMath tools are for—to help people operate more from this energetic heart zone. That's what gives people leverage over day-to-day stress triggers that would otherwise take them out and create energy drain. The energetic heart is where people are more aligned with their honesty about their deeper feelings about anything. Heart vulnerability helps create that alignment.

Understanding Makeovers

People have deeper feelings about issues and they have *makeover feelings.* You've probably heard friends say after a spat, "I'm okay, I'm fine," when they're really only half okay. That's a makeover. It's the deeper feelings that people can't change that draw the same stressors, like the next spat. A makeover doesn't create clearing. That which isn't cleared in stressful situations (especially with other people) accumulates and stores stress in the emotional nature. That stored stress has a draining effect on your mental, emotional, and physical nature. Learning to clear is the next inner frontier to explore if you want leverage over stress.

When you tell someone at the office or at home, "I'm okay" after a disagreement that still leaves stress, you have to do something with that churning energy. You might tell yourself to get some fresh air or take a walk. That may give you a moment of release or have a soothing effect that maybe lasts a day or so. But if the stress pattern is deeply ingrained, it still has to be cleared, or you'll run into the same triggers and stresses the next day. People posture and live in makeovers—everybody does. But because of the fast pace of life and more stressors in life, makeovers don't work like they used to, when people felt they could just get by. Makeovers leave too much unfriendly stored energy to be dealt with that takes a toll on your body and on your life. That's why in-the-moment techniques for stress relief and clearing as you go are more important than ever.

The Freeze-Frame Technique

Freeze-Frame is a technique that helps you slow down your mental and emotional reactions and be heart vulnerable, in the moment, in order to find a new solution to a stressful problem or issue. We use the term "Freeze-Frame" because it's a lot like pressing the pause button on your video recorder. You stop the movie of your life for a moment so you can edit the frame and create a different outcome.

With Freeze-Frame, you first take a time-out to admit what you're thinking and feeling and how you're reacting. You see where judgments or projections lurk underneath, and you take them to the heart. The next steps help get your systems in sync so you can cultivate coherence to shift the emotions and beliefs that are coloring your perceptions. The last two steps help you find new intuitive responses. From your deeper heart, you can discover a bigger picture and see which way to go.

> *Here's how Bob, a seventeen-year-old high school student, describes it: "When someone is giving me the cold shoulder and I start to judge them and get mad, I use the Freeze-Frame to stop and check it out. By Freeze-Framing before I go ballistic, my heart can tell me whether my perception is really true or just based on some previous experience. It's like a reality check. Last week I thought my friend was giving me the cold shoulder. After doing the Freeze-Frame, I saw that he was just preoccupied and that was why he wasn't noticing me."*

The following exercise will help prepare you to use the Freeze-Frame technique.

✐ Write down three things you have a buildup of stress about. They could be about work, your spouse, kids, relatives, friends, yourself, or life. They could be the issues that create the stress feelings you experience most often—the ones you listed in the previous exercise. Now write down three things that are easy for you to love, appreciate, or care about—the things that give you those uplifting feelings you experience most often. These could be people you love, special times you care about, or fun things you appreciate, where you don't have stress accounts. This is your heart coherence list.

Now pick one issue from your stress list to try out the Freeze-Frame technique. Don't pick your biggest problem for your first try. Pick something that bothers you just a little. Be heart vulnerable about it. Write a sentence or two on how the issue makes you think, feel, and react. Then pick one thing from your heart coherence list to use in step 3 of the Freeze-Frame technique.

✐ *Freeze-Frame Technique*

1. Take a time-out so that you can temporarily disengage from your thoughts and feelings, especially stressful ones. (Stop to admit how you're thinking, feeling, and reacting, then put it all on pause.)

2. Shift your focus to the area around your heart. Now feel your breath coming in through your heart and going out through your solar plexus. *Practice breathing this way a few times to ease into the technique.*

3. Make a sincere effort to activate a positive feeling. *Allow yourself to feel genuine appreciation or care for some person,*

place, or thing in your life (use your heart coherence list).

4. Ask yourself what would be an efficient, effective attitude or action that would balance your system and help release stress. *Your ability to think more clearly and objectively is enhanced based on the increased coherence you've created in steps 2 and 3. You can view the issue now from a broader, more balanced perspective. Ask yourself what you can do to help minimize future stress.*

5. Quietly sense any change in perception or feeling, and sustain it as long as you can. *Heart perceptions are often subtle. They gently suggest effective solutions that would be best for you and all concerned.*

Quick Freeze-Frame Steps

1. shift

2. activate

3. sense

Now write down your heart perceptions and feelings. Compare what your heart intelligence has to say with what you wrote before doing the Freeze-Frame technique. Which is more perceptive? Which is more emotional? Usually, heart perception is more intelligent and less emotional. This helps you see that it's your judgments that are emotional, not your real heart.

If You're Not Sure . . .

If you didn't get a heart perception, or you're unsure of what your heart is saying, Freeze-Frame whatever came to you by holding it in your heart and going through the steps again. You may have to do this a few times before you have a sense of intuitive knowing. On problems that have a lot of emotional weight, you may not get clarity right away. Be patient. Keep your energies in the heart, and your thoughts and feelings under control, while you genuinely ask your heart for a larger view. Your heart intelligence may be telling you to make an attitude shift, like *Let it go* or *Forgive* or *Have compassion, because she's doing the best she can.* Have the courage to listen to your heart. Use Attitude Breathing and the Heart Lock-In technique to instate the new attitude, and see what happens.

When to Use Freeze-Frame

Here are some examples of opportunities to use the Freeze-Frame technique to help you slow down your reactions, be heart vulnerable, do a reality check, and select more effective responses:

- when someone judges you, blames you, puts you down, or ignores you

- when you want to do something but aren't sure if it's the right move

- anytime you have an important decision to make

- anytime you want creative ideas or new answers

As you get skilled in the Freeze-Frame technique, your mind and heart will come into more alignment. The object of alignment is for the mind and heart to become buddies, with the heart being the wiser buddy that the mind learns from, finding more peace to enjoy life. Your mind also unfolds its higher creative capacities as it comes into deeper alignment with your heart.

Once you memorize the technique and have used it awhile, you'll be able to just use the Quick Freeze-Frame Steps to remind you what to do.

For deeper unresolved stress issues, advanced HeartMath clearing techniques are available in our book *Overcoming Emotional Chaos* (Jodere Group 2002). It may also be beneficial to seek professional help.

Clearing stress accounts is a choice that takes practice and commitment. You can stay in the head and be a puppet to your emotional agendas and predictable emotional reactions, which keep you in stress and misery. Or, you can go deeper in the heart and create the coherence you need to unravel the mysteries of your life, transforming stress as you go.

chapter 10

Finding Your Rhythm

People have talked and written about the importance of staying in the now or living in the moment to increase happiness. But you need your own empowerment to even keep up with now as the pace of life increases. The twentieth-century poet and monk Thomas Merton wrote, "Happiness is not a matter of intensity, but of balance and order and rhythm and harmony" (1955, 127). This comes from learning to empower in the moment and find balance and rhythm as you move through the next moments of life and the next. Learning to empower and live in the moment requires that you free yourself from judgments about the past and projections about the future. The mind and emotions tend to stay occupied with both. Being preoccupied with the past or the future creates much of your stress.

Throughout this book, you have learned a new science of rhythm through resistances that will help free you of judgments about the past and projections about the future. You have practiced scientifically validated tools and techniques to help you let go of worry, fatigue, and tension and transform stress. Now, it's important to set up a practice program to find a new rhythm to get the most out of your life and experience the joy of more stress-free living.

Setting Up a Practice Program

To start your practice program, begin with the Quick Coherence technique and practice it several times a day to establish coherence. Learn what coherence feels like to your system and how it affects the quality of communications, activities, and tasks you do every day.

Then add the Heart Lock-In technique. Practice it for five to fifteen minutes daily or several times a week in order to sustain coherence for longer periods. Regular practice of the Heart Lock-In technique will begin to restructure your emotional responses.

Next, learn and practice the Attitude Breathing tool to add the extra coherence power you need to shift out of strong negative attitudes and emotions and anchor new attitudes and hormonal states for high performance.

Finally, practice the Freeze-Frame technique to gain more understanding of your stored stress patterns and clear them for better decision making.

It's very important to learn what these different HeartMath tools and techniques feel like to your system. Each one trains you to find a more balanced and harmonious flow. Having the tools and techniques at hand is like having a best friend when you need one. They are tools and techniques of your real self.

Give Yourself Time

As you practice the techniques and tools, allow yourself some time to iron out issues in which you've invested a lot of emotional energy. You can't expect to transform a twenty-year anxiety problem that's causing you continual stress in your first five minutes of practice. However, many people have seen dramatic improvements in worry, fatigue, tension, aches and pains, and other stress symptoms after just a few days or a few weeks of practice. The more regularly you practice increasing and sustaining coherence, the sooner you will experience change. In organizational training programs, we do assessments at the end of ninety days of practice, and we've seen many ailments, from low-grade depression to high blood pressure, normalized in that time. Every person has different stress issues. What's important is not to compare yourself with others but to track your progress weekly or monthly over ninety days. Remember, progress comes in ratios. You may be surprised at how many stresses no longer get to you and how much smoother your life has become, even if some of the old stress accounts haven't cleared yet.

Keep in mind, too, that there won't be a total fix for every thing that comes up. Life doesn't always conform to people's wishes or convenience. When you face an especially sticky problem, go to the heart and apply a deeper care for all concerned, including yourself. Then you will be able to view the problem through a wider lens and more easily see what's best for everyone involved.

When things aren't changing as fast as you'd like, use Attitude Breathing and practice compassion for yourself and your challenges, but continue to move forward. If you feel like you're stuck, practice heart vulnerability with yourself or with a friend. Heart vulnerability can help you go deeper in the heart to connect with a new rhythm that brings energy and intelligence from your real self. Remember that you are building the power to reengineer your standard and predictable reactions, which in the long run will save you enormous amounts of energy and time.

Stay Genuine and Earnest

Very often, people's new self-improvement efforts dwindle once the "candy" of a breakthrough is gone or the initial high of enthusiasm wears off. Growth has rhythm and modulation to it. Progress can seem to slow down at times.

To keep yourself moving forward, stay genuine and earnest in your practice. Being genuine and being earnest are like two parts of an energy circuit that plugs you into your heart power. Genuine is a warmhearted, sincere approach. Earnest is an "I mean business" approach. These two attitudes work together to draw in more power from your spirit to help you accomplish your goals.

Being genuine will bring you more insight. Being earnest in your application of each insight keeps you on track. When you have insight and a can-do attitude, you solve, resolve, and dissolve stress. You find a rhythm that takes you past many of the challenges and resistances. Life becomes a lot more fun.

Be Prepared for the "Fade" Phenomenon

You may find that old patterns will still get in your way, causing your heart intuitions to fade. When you feel like you've slipped, don't feel bad, as that will only hold you back. Progress isn't about being perfect; it's about reconnecting with your deeper heart. It's rebooting your system when you crash, like you do your computer. It's recommitting to insights and action as soon as you notice you've faded.

The most common patterns that cause insights to fade are what we call *emotional vanity reactions,* like "I feel silly doing this," "I'm better than this," "I don't have time for this because I have more important things to do," "I'm not good enough," "I can't do this," and so forth. These thoughts and attitudes are vanity cover-ups, preventing you from getting in touch with your heart. It's not bad to have these feelings, but they will delay your progress. It's essential to release them so stress doesn't start accumulating again. Realize you are learning to take responsibility for your attitudes, and listen with integrity to your real self. If you sincerely commit to doing what your heart says, you will often get intuitive signals as reminders, just when you need them to help you follow through.

Anchor Your Insights

It's easy to have conceptual clarity about a new insight, but until the concept is anchored in feeling, it won't give you much release. That's why it's important to anchor your insights through action.

 Think back to each of the exercises you did as you worked through this book, and recall insights you had that you want to anchor. Use Attitude Breathing to anchor each insight — and the positive feeling that accompanies it — deep in your system. Throughout the day, breathe in the perception and feeling you want to remember and breathe out your intention to act on it, until the anchoring feels solid. This will give you more emotional clarity and more power to follow through.

Follow Your Heart's Intelligent Guidance

Many people make a career out of having the same insights over and over again but not really acting on them. Once you have emotional clarity, you are responsible for taking action. Following your heart is a two-part process. Part one is getting the insight or intelligence. Part two is anchoring and doing.

When you defer acting on what your heart really knows, your spirit starts to withdraw, and then life can feel harder. If this happens, just restart. Ask your heart what attitude would give you more balance and rhythm through a situation that has been causing you energy loss and anxiety. Select positive attitudes instead of rehashing something that's in the past. Ask your heart to help give you quicker access to the memory of what your heart has told you.

If something is still blocking you, use the Freeze-Frame preparation and technique, and write down your answers.

Do what your heart says, staying aligned with your spirit and real self. The power of your real spirit comes in through the power of your heart.

Cultivate a Flow of Intuition

As you practice the HeartMath tools, you will find that you are stopping energy drains at their source: your internal reactions. The more you practice engaging the power of your heart to clear your predictable reactions, the more intuitive clarity you will gain. You will start to experience a flow of intuition about how to handle everyday problems *before* you react or even in the midst of a reaction. Intuition becomes more liquid, showing you which tool to use in which situation so you can stay connected to your heart intelligence and prevent or release stress as you go.

Becoming a Rhythm Master

People often get through stressful situations by changing their rhythm. When you say, "I have to get myself together so I don't blow it," you really mean, "I have to get to the heart, even halfway, to slow down and find a new rhythm or approach." When you tell someone, "Just be calm," you are really saying, "Don't worry, take control of yourself, don't get caught up in what's going on, there is a rhythm—a way— through this." When you go to the dentist, you tell yourself, "It might hurt now, but just relax." What you're doing is trying to change an attitude so you can find a rhythm through something painful.

In contrast, when people get caught up in inner turmoil, time crunches, and incoherence, they are controlled by chaotic rhythms. Most people don't realize they can pause and shift rhythm inside to come back to balance. It's as simple as sincerely using the Quick Coherence technique. In one minute, you can be back in a more coherent and calm rhythm. You can use the Freeze-Frame technique to take a deeper look at the situation and ask your heart for intuitive guidance and direction. Especially with issues that gnaw at you, ask your heart how to restore a calm rhythm in your system or how to look at something a little more practically, without the emotional ups and downs. Going to your heart will help you stop the energy drain and find a new rhythm that feels right to you.

Becoming a rhythm master is a lot like learning to swing. When you were a child, you first started kicking and trying to make the swing go. Then someone gave you a push to help you get going and find your rhythm. (HeartMath tools give you that push to find your rhythm.) Before long, you got the feel of how and when to pump, when to shift your weight, and when to kick it up to control the speed.

Finding your rhythm takes the hard effort out of learning a new skill, whether it's self-improvement or golf or playing the piano. Once you get the feel of the new rhythm, you know how to finesse, and you keep refining your skills to improve. It's no different when you're learning to transform stress. Each time you shift attitude and rhythm and choose not to go to your old predictable way of reacting, you find new emotional flexibility for the next challenge.

The Rhythm of Fun

Real fun comes as you learn to shift rhythm toward more calm and ease. That's what helps you to avoid taking stressful situations too personally and to laugh at yourself even when you botch something. Learning the rhythm of following your heart is fun—a new, "intelligent" fun. When you know that you can always pull out a HeartMath tool to find rhythm through a resistance, you have the security to observe the process without judging yourself. You start perceiving the ups and downs as more of a dance. When you stumble or get out of step, you can dance in place a few steps to recalibrate to the rhythm so you can move forward again in step. If you see a better way to go, take the lead. Act from the energetic heart, feel it, and you will increase your effectiveness. You'll be so glad you did. Remember, what we mean by rhythm is that you either clunk through situations creating more resistance and angst, or you find the rhythm through resistance, which de-stresses the process. Your heart's intelligent guidance is designed to give you this option.

Slow Down Emotions to Speed Up Your Intelligence

Developing the power to slow your reactions allows you to move through chaotic or hectic scenarios in life with more coherence. Practice the Freeze-Frame technique to slow your reactions and find your heart more quickly when you have to make high-speed decisions. As Jim Moore, a consultant and HeartMath trainer for Hewlett-Packard, says,

> My philosophy has always been, "If it's not something I can do anything about, then I'm not going to worry." But that's mostly a mental process. The Freeze-Frame technique combines the heart. I think it's much more powerful. It helped me change my unsuccessful attempts to push my son to better grades. The technique can actually slow time so you see things a little more clearly. It's tapping into heart values, accessing all your intelligence.

By learning to sustain heart coherence, you speed up consciousness so you can slow down emotions and direct them. Over the course of a week, this practice yields a lot of saved time and energy. If you stop leaking time and energy about just two or three things, you'll find yourself feeling more buoyant and energized. You'll develop the inner power to sort through high-speed incoming information, deal with emotional intensity and weight, and handle the pace of the world around you. Don't try to be perfect; just go for improving your ratios of energy gain to energy loss. Make it fun.

The Freeze-Framer Monitor

The Freeze-Framer is a heart rhythm coherence monitor that provides objective feedback of your heart rhythm patterns. It allows you to see in real time how stressful emotions and thoughts are affecting your heart rhythms. It does this by measuring the beat-to-beat changes in heart rate, or heart rate variability. It displays your heart rhythm pattern on your computer screen while the software tutorial guides you through the Quick Coherence technique. You can watch your heart rhythms change in real time from incoherent to coherent. Three fun games that operate by your emotional control (rather than motor skill control) help build your coherence skills. There are four challenge levels, so you keep increasing your coherence abilities. The software displays your coherence level and tells you when you enter the "zone" of high performance.

The Freeze-Framer software takes you past the guesswork and gives you real data that verifies when your heart rhythms are in coherence. You learn to make small inner moves and adjustments to see how to increase and sustain coherence. Then you apply those same coherence-building inner moves in your daily activities.

The Freeze-Framer is used by health-care professionals, therapists, and coaches to help clients reduce stress and improve mental, emotional, or physical health and also performance. Athletes train with it to get in the "zone" and improve performance in competition. Students use it to improve test scores. Police officers use it to release stress, renew their energy, and recalibrate their responses, especially after encountering dangerous situations. Business leaders use it to relieve stress and improve health and decision making.

> *Dave holds an executive position with a national trade association. "When I purchased the Freeze-Framer software from HeartMath, I was having irregular heartbeats and severe anxiety attacks. I'd actually developed a fear of anxiety attacks that made me get sucked into them sooner than when I first began experiencing them. They were affecting my work performance. I learned to manage both of those anxiety events, physical and emotional, with regular use of the Freeze-Framer."*

The Heart's Electromagnetic Field

The heart's powerful electromagnetic field affects emotional interactions between people. Your heart rhythms have an impact on others. The electromagnetic signal produced by your heart rhythms can literally be measured in the brain waves of people around you (McCraty 2002). So as you find a new rhythm, you help others do the same. As you learn to let go of judgments and projections and make peace with situations you can't change, you increase the coherence in your own electromagnetic field, which can be felt by the people around you and can facilitate change in them, too.

Practicing more genuine care in your interactions with others will boost your energy level and create more balance in the energetic field of your household, workplace, or any place where you gather with others. Using the HeartMath tools will help you ride the waves of change within and around you.

The Transformative Power
of the Heart

As stress and chaos continue to increase in the world, more people will come to realize that the solution to stress is to roll up their sleeves and go deep in the heart to make the difference in their own fulfillment, instead of depending on others to bring that about. As more people learn the science of the heart to transform stress and find a new rhythm of approach, we will move from the age of information overload to the age of intuition.

Research just published at the time of the writing of this book has found that not only does the heart receive and respond to intuitive information before the brain, the heart also has intuitive access to a field of information not bound by time and space (McCraty, Atkinson, and Bradley 2004a, 2004b). The heart appears to function like a radio receiver tuned to an intuitive bandwidth.

Many people will get an energetic understanding of what this means from intuitive intelligence while the scientific research is still being unfolded. As people open their hearts more, emotional understanding will bring them insights before science is able to explain the whole process. As the pace of life quickens, an upside will be a faster emotional transfer of intelligence between people that won't have to wait for what science says. This is similar to the way many people have delved into complementary and alternative medicine because intuitively they knew it offered something worthwhile, even though researchers are only now understanding why some of it works.

The intent of this book has been to help people learn to create their own way out of stress, rather than waiting for something outside of themselves to provide the quick fix. Discovering the new frontiers of peace is an inside job. It's an individual process from which the collective whole benefits.

It's time to rely on individual responsibility, which comes from being more responsible for your own energies. This can be achieved through heart intelligence, and the rewards will become more obvious through the adventure.

As you relieve stress by connecting with your heart intelligence, you will find that old emotional habits do get transformed into positive intuitive feelings and dynamic, creative energy, and that your energetic heart is the transformer — in all senses of the word. It transforms emotional energy into clarity and effectiveness.

The power and intelligence of the heart is what gives people control of their automatic responses so they recover more quickly and enjoy increased energy. It's through the power of the heart that they feel better and do better. It's also through the power of the heart that they access the higher intelligence that increasingly perceives what's best for all concerned.

This power of the heart is a new discovery for science, although it's been a part of most cultural and spiritual traditions for ages. Now that science has confirmed that the heart plays a significant role in emotional management, in efficient brain function, and in the processing and decoding of intuitive information, the hope for the twenty-first century is that people everywhere will learn to connect with that power they already have inside. This can bring to us all a higher quality of life, new hope, and — above all — increased joy and fulfillment.

Learn More about HeartMath

Explore other HeartMath books, learning programs, music, software, and professional training to reinforce and advance what you've learned in this book. More details can be found online at www.heartmathstore.com.

Books and Learning Programs by Doc Childre

Childre, Doc, and Deborah Rozman. 2003. *Transforming Anger: The HeartMath Solution for Letting Go of Rage, Frustration, and Irritation.* Oakland, Calif.: New Harbinger Publications.

Childre, Doc, and Deborah Rozman. 2002. *Overcoming Emotional Chaos: Eliminate Anxiety, Lift Depression, and Create Security in Your Life.* San Diego: Jodere Group.

Childre, Doc, and Howard Martin. 1999. *The HeartMath Solution.* San Francisco: HarperSanFrancisco.

Childre, Doc, and Bruce Cryer. 2000. *From Chaos to Coherence: The Power to Change Performance.* Boulder Creek, Calif.: Planetary Publications.

Childre, Doc. 1998. *Freeze-Frame: A Scientifically Proven Technique for Clear Decision Making and Improved Health.* Boulder Creek, Calif.: Planetary Publications.

Childre, Doc. 1996. *Teaching Children to Love: 80 Games and Fun Activities for Raising Balanced Children in Unbalanced Times.* Boulder Creek, Calif.: Planetary Publications.

Childre, Doc. 1992. *The How to Book of Teen Self Discovery.* Boulder Creek, Calif.: Planetary Publications.

From Chaos to Coherence (CD-ROM). HeartMath LLC: Boulder Creek, Calif. and Knowledgebuilder.com.

Freeze-Frame Learning Program (CD-ROM). Boulder Creek, Calif.: Planetary Publications.

Music by Doc Childre

These recordings are scientifically designed to enhance the practice of HeartMath techniques and tools.

Heart Zones. 1991. Planetary Publications.

Speed of Balance. 1996. Planetary Publications.

Quiet Joy. 2001. Planetary Publications.

Freeze-Framer Monitor
created by Doc Childre

The Freeze-Framer interactive learning system, with a patented heart rhythm monitor and three software games, allows you to observe your heart rhythms in real time and assists you in shifting into coherence and sustaining coherence (the "zone" of high performance).

HeartMath Training, Seminars, and Telecourses

HeartMath provides world-class training programs for organizations, hospitals, health-care providers, and individuals. HeartMath training is available through on-site programs, licensing and certification for organizations, sponsored workshops, seminars, conference presentations, and telephone courses.

Licensing and Certification: Training to Become a One-on-One Provider

HeartMath offers licensing and certification to health-care providers and coaches wanting to use HeartMath tools and technology as part of the services they provide to clients in a one-on-one professional setting.

For information on products, training, and coaching programs, call (800) 450-9111, e-mail info@heartmath.com, visit the Web site at www.heartmath.com, or write to HeartMath, 14700 West Park Avenue, Boulder Creek, CA 95006.

Research and Education

The Institute of HeartMath (IHM) is a nonprofit research and education organization dedicated to understanding emotions and the role of the heart in learning, performance, and well-being. IHM offers two programs for use in educational and classroom settings:

> *TestEdge* programs for improving academic performance and test scores

Teacher Resiliency programs for teachers, administrators, and principals

---

For information about Institute of HeartMath research initiatives and education programs, call (831) 338-8500, e-mail info@heartmath.org, visit the Web site at www.heartmath.org, or write to Institute of HeartMath, 14700 West Park Avenue, Boulder Creek, CA 95006.

Stress Freedom United

Stress Freedom United is a national nonprofit consumer organization dedicated to helping consumers control stress, enhance personal performance, and make the world a better place to live and work. Its goals are to:

- Provide consumers with a national organization to turn to for information and support

- Empower consumers to seek policy and legal changes that will make life and work less stressful

- Support on-going and new research designed to cure and control stress

For more information visit **www.stressfreedom.org.**

Scientific Monographs

For an in-depth discussion of the Institute of HeartMath's research, see IHM's scientific monographs, published as e-booklets and available on the Institute of HeartMath Web site: www.heartmath.org. Summaries are available online.

Armour, J. Andrew. 2003. *Neurocardiology — Anatomical and Functional Principles*. Boulder Creek, Calif.: Institute of HeartMath.

McCraty, Rollin. 2002. *The Energetic Heart: Bioelectromagnetic Interactions within and between People.* Boulder Creek, Calif.: Institute of HeartMath.

McCraty, Rollin. 2003. *Heart-Brain Neurodynamics: The Making of Emotions.* Boulder Creek, Calif.: Institute of HeartMath.

McCraty, Rollin, and Doc Childre. 2002. *The Appreciative Heart: The Psychophysiology of Positive Emotions and Optimal Functioning.* Boulder Creek, Calif.: Institute of HeartMath.

McCraty, Rollin, and Mike Atkinson. 2003. *Psychophysiological Coherence.* Boulder Creek, Calif.: Institute of HeartMath.

McCraty, Rollin, Mike Atkinson, and Dana Tomasino. 2001. *Science of the Heart: Exploring the Role of the Heart in Human Performance.* Boulder Creek, Calif.: Institute of HeartMath.

See also: McCraty, Rollin. 2002. Heart rhythm coherence — An emerging area of biofeedback. *Biofeedback* 30(1):23–25.

References

Arguelles, L., R. McCraty, and R. A. Rees. 2003. The heart in holistic education. *Encounter: Education for Meaning and Social Justice* 16(3):13–21.

Armour, J. A. 2003. *Neurocardiology – Anatomical and Functional Principles.* Boulder Creek, Calif.: HeartMath Research Center, Institute of HeartMath, Publication No. 03-011.

Arnsten, A. F. T. 1998. The biology of being frazzled. *Science* 280(5370):1711–12.

Bacon, S. L., L. L. Watkins, M. Babyak, A. Sherwood, J. Hayano, A. L. Hinderliter, R. Waugh, A. Georgiades, and J. A. Blumenthal. 2004. The effects of daily stress on autonomic cardiac control in coronary artery disease patients. *Psychosomatic Medicine* 66(1):A15 (Online supplement: www.psychosomaticmedicine.org/cgi/data/66/1/DC1/1).

Baker, D., and C. Smith. 2003. *What Happy People Know: How the New Science of Happiness Can Change Your Life for the Better.* Emmaus, Pa.: Rodale.

Becker, D. M., G. Wand, L. R. Yanek, T. F. Moy, B. G. Kral, I. Wittstein, R. S. Blumenthal, and L. C. Becker. 2003. Reactivity to mental stress predicts future coronary disease events in families at high risk for premature coronary disease in the Johns Hopkins Sibling Study. Paper presented at the American Heart Association Scientific Sessions 2003, Orlando, Fla., November 9–12.

Bellavere, F. 1995. Heart rate variability in patients with diabetes and other noncardiological diseases. In *Heart Rate Variability*, edited by M. Malik and A. J. Camm, 507–16. Armonk, N.Y.: Futura Publishing Company.

Cavigelli, S. A., and M. K. McClintock. 2003. Fear of novelty in infant rats predicts adult corticosterone dynamics and an early death. *Proceedings of the National Academy of Sciences USA* 100(26):16131–36.

Childre, D., and B. Cryer. 2000. *From Chaos to Coherence: The Power to Change Performance*. Boulder Creek, Calif.: Planetary Publications.

Cobain, M. R. 2002. A psycho-social intervention in the workplace: Endocrine and cardiovascular effects. Unilever R&D Colworth, Research Report CW 02 0319, December.

Cohen, S., D. A. Tyrrell, and A. P. Smith. 1991. Psychological stress and susceptibility to the common cold. *New England Journal of Medicine* 325(9):606–12.

Colino, S. 2004. Take control of stress this second. *Cosmopolitan*, May: 214–18.

Davidson, R. J., J. Kabat-Zinn, J. Schumacher, M. Rosenkranz, D. Muller, S. F. Santorelli, F. Urbanowski, A. Harrington, K. Bonus, and J. F. Sheridan. 2003. Alterations in brain and immune function produced by mindfulness meditation. *Psychosomatic Medicine* 65(4):564–70.

Dekker, J. M., E. G. Schouten, P. Klootwijk, J. Pool, C. A. Swenne, and D. Kromhout. 1997. Heart rate variability from short electrocardiographic recordings predicts mortality from all causes in middle-aged and elderly men. The Zutphen Study. *American Journal of Epidemiology* 145(10): 899–908.

Eysenck, H. J. 1988. Personality, stress and cancer: Prediction and prophylaxis. *British Journal of Medical Psychology* 61(Pt 1):57–75.

Flegal, K. M., M. D. Carroll, C. L. Ogden, and C. L. Johnson. 2002. Prevalence and trends in obesity among U.S. adults, 1999–2000. *Journal of the American Medical Association* 288(14):1723–27.

Frysinger, R. C., and R. M. Harper. 1990. Cardiac and respiratory correlations with unit discharge in epileptic human temporal lobe. *Epilepsia* 31(2):162–71.

Gershon, M. 1999. *The Second Brain.* San Francisco: HarperCollins.

Gibbs, W. W. 2004. Why machines should fear. *Scientific American* 290(1):37–37A.

Grossarth-Maticek, R., and H. J. Eysenck. 1995. Self-regulation and mortality from cancer, coronary heart disease and other causes: A prospective study. *Personality and Individual Differences* 19(6):781–95.

Haggin Geary, L. 2003. I quit! Overworked employees are fed up: A survey finds 8 out of 10 Americans want a new job. *CNN/Money,* December 30. http://money.cnn.com/2003/11/11/pf/q_iquit/?cnn=yes.

Harris Interactive. 2002. *Tension Tracker 2002: Report of Findings.* Fort Washington, Pa.: McNeil Consumer & Specialty Pharmaceuticals.

Horackova, M. 2004. Colocalization of multiple neurochemicals in mammalian intrathoracic neurons. In *Basic and Clinical Neurocardiology,* edited by J. A. Armour and J. L. Ardell, 61–78. New York: Oxford University Press.

Huang, M. H., J. Ebey, and S. Wolf. 1989. Responses of the QT interval of the electrocardiogram during emotional stress. *Psychosomatic Medicine* 51(4):419–27.

International Health, Racquet & Sportsclub Association. 2004. Obesity level in U.S. to hit 40% by 2010. *Club Business International,* March, 30, 32.

Kawachi, I., D. Sparrow, P. S. Vokonas, and S. T. Weiss. 1994. Symptoms of anxiety and risk of coronary heart disease. The Normative Aging Study. *Circulation* 90(5):2225–29.

Kiecolt-Glaser, J. K., R. Glaser, S. Gravenstein, W. B. Malarkey, and J. Sheridan. 1996. Chronic stress alters the immune response to influenza virus vaccine in older adults. *Proceedings of the National Academy of Sciences USA* 93(7):3043–47.

Lupien, S. J., M. de Leon, S. de Santi, A. Convit, C. Tarshish, N. P. Nair, M. Thakur, B. S. McEwen, R. L. Hauger, and M. J. Meaney. 1998. Cortisol levels during human aging predict hippocampal atrophy and memory deficits. *Nature Neuroscience* 1(1):69–73.

Luskin, F., M. Reitz, K. Newell, T. G. Quinn, and W. Haskell. 2002. A controlled pilot study of stress management training of elderly patients with congestive heart failure. *Preventive Cardiology* 5(4):168–72, 176.

McCraty, R. 2002. *The Energetic Heart: Bioelectromagnetic Interactions within and between People.* Boulder Creek, Calif.: HeartMath Research Center, Institute of HeartMath, Publication No. 02-035.

McCraty, R. 2003. *Heart-Brain Neurodynamics: The Making of Emotions.* Boulder Creek, Calif.: HeartMath Research Center, Institute of HeartMath, Publication No. 03-015.

McCraty, R. 2004. The energetic heart: Bioelectromagnetic communication within and between people. In *Bioelectromagnetic Medicine,* edited by P. J. Rosch and M. S. Markov, 541–62. New York: Marcel Dekker.

McCraty, R., and M. Atkinson. 2003. *Psychophysiological Coherence.* Boulder Creek, Calif.: HeartMath Research Center, Institute of HeartMath, Publication 03-016.

McCraty, R., M. Atkinson, and R. T. Bradley. 2004a. Electrophysiological evidence of intuition: Part 1. The surprising role of the heart. *Journal of Alternative and Complementary Medicine* 10(1):133–43.

McCraty, R., M. Atkinson, and R. T. Bradley. 2004b. Electrophysiological evidence of intuition: Part 2. A system-wide process? *Journal of Alternative and Complementary Medicine* 10(2):325–36.

McCraty, R., M. Atkinson, and L. Lipsenthal. 2000. *Emotional self-regulation program enhances psychological health and quality of life in patients with diabetes.* Boulder Creek, Calif.: HeartMath Research Center, Institute of HeartMath, Publication No. 00-006.

McCraty, R., M. Atkinson, G. Rein, and A. D. Watkins. 1996. Music enhances the effect of positive emotional states on salivary IgA. *Stress Medicine* 12(3):167–75.

McCraty, R., M. Atkinson, W. A. Tiller, G. Rein, and A. D. Watkins. 1995. The effects of emotions on short-term heart rate variability using power spectrum analysis. *American Journal of Cardiology* 76(14):1089–93.

McCraty, R., M. Atkinson, and D. Tomasino. 2003. Impact of a workplace stress reduction program on blood pressure and emotional health in hypertensive employees. *Journal of Alternative and Complementary Medicine* 9(3):355–69.

McCraty, R., M. Atkinson, D. Tomasino, and W. A. Tiller. 1998. The electricity of touch: Detection and measurement of cardiac energy exchange between people. In *Brain and Values: Is a Biological Science of Values Possible?* edited by K. H. Pribram, 359–79. Mahwah, N.J.: Lawrence Erlbaum Associates, Publishers.

McCraty, R., B. Barrios-Choplin, D. Rozman, M. Atkinson, and A. D. Watkins. 1998. The impact of a new emotional self-management program on stress, emotions, heart rate variability, DHEA and cortisol. *Integrative Physiological and Behavioral Science* 33(2):151–70.

McCraty, R., and D. Childre. 2002. *The Appreciative Heart: The Psychophysiology of Positive Emotions and Optimal Functioning.* Boulder Creek, Calif.: HeartMath Research Center, Institute of HeartMath, Publication No. 02-026.

McCraty, R., and D. Childre. 2004. The grateful heart: The psychophysiology of appreciation. In *The Psychology of Gratitude,* edited by R. A. Emmons and M. E. McCullough, 230–55. New York: Oxford University Press.

McCraty, R., S. Lanson, and M. Atkinson. 1997. Assessment of autonomic function and balance in chronic fatigue patients using 24-hour heart rate variability analysis. *Clinical Autonomic Research* 7(5):237.

Melton, L. 2004. Aching atrophy: More than unpleasant, chronic pain shrinks the brain. *Scientific American* 290(1): 22–24.

Merton, T. 1955. *No Man Is an Island.* New York: Harcourt Brace.

Merritt, R. 2004. New insight into effects of daily stresses on heart health. *DukeMed News,* March 4. http://dukemednews.org/news/article.php?id=7432.

Morse, S. 2004. Emotion rules! *Washington Post,* March 23, HE04.

Namiki, M. 1994. Aged people and stress. *Japanese Journal of Geriatrics* 31(2):85–95.

NDCHealth. 2003. *PharmaTrends: 2002 Year in Review – U.S. Market.* New York: NDCHealth.

Parker, L. N., E. R. Levin, and E. T. Lifrak. 1985. Evidence for adrenocortical adaptation to severe illness. *Journal of Clinical Endocrinology and Metabolism* 60(5):947–52.

Raikkonen, K., K. A. Matthews, and K. Salomon. 2003. Hostility predicts metabolic syndrome risk factors in children and adolescents. *Health Psychology* 22(3):279–86.

Rein, G., M. Atkinson, and R. McCraty. 1995. The physiological and psychological effects of compassion and anger. *Journal of Advancement in Medicine* 8(2):87–105.

Rosch, P. J. 1991. Job stress: America's leading adult health problem. *USA Today*, May:42–44.

Rosch, P. J., and C. C. Clark. 2001. *De-Stress, Weigh Less*. New York: St. Martin's Press.

Ross, E., and J. B. Verrengia. 2004. Obesity becoming major global problem. *Associated Press*, May 8.

Rozman, D., R. Whitaker, T. Beckman, and D. Jones. 1996. A pilot intervention program which reduces psychological symptomatology in individuals with human immunodeficiency virus. *Complementary Therapies in Medicine* 4(4):226–32.

Sapolsky, R. M. 1996. Why stress is bad for your brain. *Science* 273(5276):749–50.

Sedona Training Associates. 2004. Survey reveals antidepressant drug users 5 times more likely to consider suicide; 57% continue to suffer from depression. *PR Newswire*, March 31.

Shealy, C. N. 1995. A review of dehydroepiandrosterone (DHEA). *Integrative Physiological and Behavioral Science* 30(4):308–13.

Simon Silver, C. 2003. Worried sick: The high price of being fearful. *Genome News Network*, December 24. www. genomenewsnetwork.org/articles/12_03/novelty.shtml.

Singer, D. H., and Z. Ori. 1995. Changes in heart rate variability associated with sudden cardiac death. In *Heart Rate Variability*, edited by M. Malik and A. J. Camm, 429–48. Armonk, N.Y.: Futura Publishing Company.

Tiller, W. A., R. McCraty, and M. Atkinson. 1996. Cardiac coherence: A new, noninvasive measure of autonomic nervous system order. *Alternative Therapies in Health and Medicine* 2(1):52–65.

Vybiral, T., and D. H. Glaeser. 1995. Changes of heart rate variability preceding ventricular arrhythmias. In *Heart Rate Variability*, edited by M. Malik and A. J. Camm, 421–28. Armonk, N.Y.: Futura Publishing Company.

Doc Childre is the founder and chairman of the scientific advisory board of the Institute of HeartMath, the chairman of HeartMath, LLC, and the chairman and co-CEO of Quantum Intech, Inc. He is the author of eight books and a consultant to business leaders, scientists, educators, and the entertainment industry on Intui-Technology®. His HeartMath® System and proprietary heart rhythm technology for coherence building, called the *Freeze-Framer®,* has been featured in USA Today, Wall Street Journal, New York Times, *Los Angeles Times*, NBC Today Show, ABC Good Morning America, ABC World News Tonight, CNN Headline News, CNN.com, *Harvard Business Review, Business 2.0, Newsweek, Industry Week, Prevention, Psychology Today, Golf Magazine, Self, New Woman magazine, Men's Fitness, Army Times,* and numerous other publications around the world.

Deborah Rozman, Ph.D., is a high performance psychologist with thirty years of experience as an educator and business executive and the author of six books. She is President and co-CEO of Quantum Intech, overseeing the expansion of HeartMath® worldwide. Quantum Intech develops and licenses products and services that reduce stress, improve health, and increase performance based on the HeartMath® System. Deborah also serves on the Institute of HeartMath's scientific advisory board and Physics of Humanity council. She is a key spokesperson for the HeartMath® System, giving media interviews and keynote addresses for executives, scientists, and health professionals throughout the world.

Some Other New Harbinger Titles

The Diabetes Lifestyle Book, Item 5167 $16.95

Solid to the Core, Item 4305 $14.95

Staying Focused in the Age of Distraction, Item 433X $16.95

Living Beyond Your Pain, Item 4097 $19.95

Fibromyalgia & Chronic Fatigue Syndrome, Item 4593 $14.95

Your Miraculous Back, Item 4526 $18.95

TriEnergetics, Item 4453 $15.95

Emotional Fitness for Couples, Item 4399 $14.95

The MS Workbook, Item 3902 $19.95

Depression & Your Thyroid, Item 4062 $15.95

The Eating Wisely for Hormonal Balance Journal,
     Item 3945 $15.95

Healing Adult Acne, Item 4151 $15.95

The Memory Doctor, Item 3708 $11.95

The Emotional Wellness Way to Cardiac Health, Item 3740 $16.95

The Cyclothymia Workbook, Item 383X $18.95

The Matrix Repatterning Program for Pain Relief, Item 3910 $18.95

Transforming Stress, Item 397X $10.95

Eating Mindfully, Item 3503 $13.95

Living with RSDS, Item 3554 $16.95

The Ten Hidden Barriers to Weight Loss, Item 3244 $11.95

Call **toll free, 1-800-748-6273,** or log on to our online bookstore at **www.newharbinger.com** to order. Have your Visa or Mastercard number ready. Or send a check for the titles you want to New Harbinger Publications, Inc., 5674 Shattuck Ave., Oakland, CA 94609. Include $4.50 for the first book and 75¢ for each additional book, to cover shipping and handling. (California residents please include appropriate sales tax.) Allow two to five weeks for delivery.

Prices subject to change without notice.